Web of Meaning

A Developmental-Contextual Approach in Sexual Abuse Treatment

Gail Ryan
and Associates

KEMPE CHILDREN'S CENTER
UNIVERSITY OF COLORADO HEALTH SCIENCES CENTER
DENVER, COLORADO

Safer Society Press
PO BOX 340 • BRANDON • VT 05733

Gail Ryan is grateful for the input and support of the clinical staff of the Kempe Center and numerous colleagues in the original presentation of Chapter 1. This paper was presented at the 17th annual Child Abuse and Neglect Symposium, June 1988, Keystone, Colorado. It is reprinted here with permission from the Journal of Interpersonal Violence, *vol. 4, no. 3, September 1989, pp. 325–341, Sage Publications, Inc.*

Developmental Editor: Euan Bear

Cover design: Laura Augustine
Production management: Jenna Dixon, Bookbuilder
Copyeditor: Linda Lotz
Typesetting: Sam Sheng, CompuDesign
Proofreader: Beth Richards
Printing: Malloy Lithographing, Inc.

ISBN 1-884444-50-4
$22.00
Bulk discounts available.
Order from:

Safer Society Press
P.O. Box 340
Brandon, VT 05733
802-247-3132
Phone orders welcome with Visa or MasterCard.

Library of Congress Cataloging-in-Publication Data
Ryan, Gail.
    Web of meaning : a developmental-contextual approach in sexual treatment / Gail Ryan and associates.
        p.   cm.
    Includes bibliographical references and index.
    ISBN 1-884444-50-4 (alk. paper)
    1. Adult child sexual abuse victims. 2. Child sexual abuse. 3. Sexually abused children. I. Title.
RC569.5.A28R9   1999
616.85'836—dc21   98-30615

08 07 06 05 04 03 02 01 00 99   10 9 8 7 6 5 4 3 2 1   1st Printing 1999

Dedication
To Brandt Steele … "the wind beneath our wings."

KEMPE STUDY GROUP
On the Development of Offending and Long-Term Dysfunction in
Sexual Abuse Victims
1987–1997

Gail Ryan, M.A., Facilitator
Director, Perpetration Prevention Program, Kempe Center;
Senior Instructor, Department of Pediatrics, University of
Colorado Health Sciences Center

MEMBERS[†]
Lynda Arnold, L.C.S.W., private practice
Carol Bilbrey, L.C.S.W., Myron Stratton Home, Colorado Springs
John Dick, L.C.S.W., Myron Stratton Home, Colorado Springs
Tim Fuente, M.S.W., L.C.S.W. II, Fuente & Wand
Candace Grosz, M.S.W., Third Party Project, Kempe Center
Debra Grove, Ph.D., private practice
Carol Haase, M.P.A., Third Party Project, Kempe Center
Phil Hyden, M.D., The Violence Intervention Program, University of
   Southern California Medical Center, Los Angeles County
Gizane Indart, M.A., Namaqua Center, Loveland, Colorado
Connie Isaac, R.S.A., Inc.
Ruth Kempe, M.D., Third Party Project, Kempe Center
Laurie Knight, B.A., a local county social services agency
Sandy Lane, R.N., R.S.A., Inc.
Barry R. Lindstrom, Ph.D., Namaqua Center, Loveland, Colorado
Jeff Metzner, M.D., Young Sexual Offenders Treatment Program, Kempe
   Center
Scott Plejdrup, Keepsafe Project, Kempe Center
Courtney Pullen, M.A., L.P.C., MASA (Males Affected by Sexual Abuse)
Emili Rambus, Psy.D., private practice
Lindsay March Schweitzer, M.A., Keepsafe Project, Kempe Center
Brandt Steele, M.D., Kempe Center, University of Colorado Health
   Sciences Center
Bob Wagstaff, M.A., A.C.S.W., Myron Stratton Home, Colorado Springs
Sherri Wand, M.S.W., L.S.W. II, Fuente & Wand
Jerry Yager, Psy.D., Denver Children's Home

[†]Affiliations listed for the period of involvement in the Kempe Study Group.

Contents

Illustrations

Preface

Maltreatment of children has been known for millennia in the forms of incest, infanticide, neglect, abandonment, and orphanage. Nonaccidental (inflicted) trauma has become a significant subject of concern only in the recent past. It began in the 1950s with studies of fractures and subdural hematomas, followed by rapidly increasing numbers of reports in the 1960s of other types of physical abuse in the form of the "battered child syndrome." Not until the 1970s did case reports of sexual abuse become as common as reports of physical abuse.

In recent years an almost overwhelming plethora of books, professional journal articles, and case studies of sexual abuse has developed, along with abundant discussions in the public media. Various perspectives have been published by pediatricians, psychiatrists, psychologists, gynecologists, sociobiologists, social workers, legal experts, law enforcement personnel, and victim/survivors of abuse. This literature deals with etiology, symptoms, diagnosis, and treatment, as well as demographics, case management, civil and criminal prosecution, and the immediate and long-term residues and outcomes of sexual abuse. Both clinical case studies and more rigid empirical and statistical studies of various facets of abuse and of various theories and modalities of treatment are abundant. The problem of how best to deal with all this information and provide therapy is a daunting one.

The present volume is rather different in that it presents a basis for the therapist involved in daily work to try to understand how the client got where he/she is today and how best to help him/her cope with the astounding complexity of intellectual and emotional responses to life experiences, especially that of being sexually abused. Philosophically, our group has followed four basic assumptions:

1. Each person is a unique individual who has a unique life experience.

2. Development is epigenic, each phase building on previous stages and involving constant interaction between genetic endowment and experience.

3. Experience begins at birth in the interaction between infant and whatever primary caregiver fate has provided for attachment.

4. In relationship with the attachment figure, the infant develops an internal working model of what the world is like and how best to adapt to it in order to live.

To bring some order to all the available data, a guide, called a matrix, was developed as a kind of map or outline of how the many facts and variables of life experience can be related to one another and organized to achieve the best understanding of clients in order to help them.

Residues of early attachment patterns developed in infancy with primary caregivers persist into adult life. Many years ago, in chatting with a younger colleague, we found that both of us had been involved in World War II: he as a young marine in the first wave of men going through the surf to invade Japanese-held land in the Pacific, and I as a psychiatrist in a medical unit going with the 1st and 9th Armies from Normandy through France and Belgium into Germany. I remarked that his experience was even worse than mine and that he must have been terrified walking into Japanese gunfire. He said, "No, I wasn't afraid." I was surprised by his response and asked, "Weren't you afraid you'd be killed when you saw your buddies falling wounded or dead around you?" He thought a moment and then replied, "No, I knew my mother wouldn't allow it." What a wonderful guardian angel to have as part of one's internal working model!

The four basic assumptions noted above apply to therapists as well as to clients. We must always be aware of our own life experiences and the biases and beliefs that can interfere with our understanding of and responses to our clients' stories. Even the words we use can mean something quite different to our clients. We must be flexible, sensitive, and able to adapt to the focus and emotional status of clients, which can change abruptly from week to week and catch us off guard.

In a sense, this book is an effort to counteract the normal human tendency toward reduction and oversimplification of complex problems with the hope of making treatment easier. We know that the luxury of time to fully explore the depths and visualization of people's lives is not always available in our current mental health care environment. The constraints of managed care and insurance limits encourage or necessitate the use of quick fixes or Band-Aid approaches to treat complex human problems. Even so, awareness of the uniqueness of each individual can aid the therapist's ability to provide differential diagnoses and treatments with carefully selected goals and objectives.

—*Brandt Steele, M.D.*

Introduction

We're not really experts ... just curious people, trying to understand how we can help the people we treat to be a little less unhappy.

— Brandt Steele, M.D.

For many years, the Kempe National Center for the Prevention and Treatment of Child Abuse and Neglect has maintained an interest in the exploration of the developmental pathways of victims, perpetrators, and survivors of sexual abuse. One effort has been the ongoing study group of diverse clinicians from a variety of Colorado treatment settings who began meeting in 1987 to explore the following question:

> When we have a whole group of individuals who experience sexual abuse in childhood, and we see that as adults, some of these individuals experience sexual dysfunctions, some experience nonsexual dysfunctions, and others do not experience any dysfunction, how can we understand who is at risk for which type of outcome, and how can we reduce the risk of dysfunctional outcomes for those we treat?

The group's attention to this question was sparked by a draft of the journal article "Victim to Victimizer: Rethinking Victim Treatment" (Ryan, 1989), which hypothesized that a dysfunctional pattern of coping with the experience of abuse might be evident in the symptoms of child victims and subsequently evolve into the disorders described by older survivors and perpetrators of sexual abuse. That paper is reprinted here as Chapter 1.

The concepts set forth in that paper met with mixed reactions from colleagues in the field. Some clinicians treating victims resisted the notion that their clients might continue to be at risk of becoming perpetrators despite the therapy they had received, while others were very aware of these risks and were excited by the paper. Reviewers of the paper were understandably hesitant to publish a purely theoretical paper without some empirical justification, yet with some of the earliest victims who had received treatment already returning to treatment centers as youthful offenders (or with other dangerous behaviors), it seemed reasonable to pose the questions — even if the answers were still unclear. Local colleagues who were stimulated to explore these issues accepted an invitation to meet to study the question, and the Kempe Study Group was formed.

Chapter 2 summarizes the work (1987–1989) of the original members of the group. The membership of this group has changed over the years, as some colleagues have moved away or been unable to attend and new associates have asked to participate. However, membership has always included clinicians representing work with all ages and both sexes of victims, perpetrators, and survivors in diverse treatment settings — outpatient, residential, individual, group, and family. The group has been a rich source of stimulation and support for its members, a fertile ground from which many of the concepts of the Kempe Center's Perpetration Prevention Program have grown.

Throughout the first decade of work with childhood sexual abuse, sexual victimization was viewed as different from other types of child abuse, and intervention and research represented a specialty. Even within the sexual abuse field, child victims, adult survivors, and sexual abusers were viewed in isolation from one another and from other clinical populations. The professional tendency to view sexual abuse in a discrete and controlled manner parallels the process of the clients, helping everyone involved to feel some sense of "containment" in order to manage their thoughts about an abhorrent phenomenon. By bringing together a group of diverse clinicians from the different subspecialties, containment was challenged and a process of integration began. The implications of the questions posed in Chapter 1 and the conceptual hypotheses developed in Chapter 2 have influenced the clinical practice of the clinicians in the group by demanding that sexual abuse be viewed in a more holistic context and that treatment be tailored to the unique phenomenology of the individual client.

The rest of the chapters were written by current members of the study group in order to share with colleagues some of the beliefs, experiences, and practices that have evolved from the process of this group and the clinical experience of its members. The book does not replace the excellent textbooks and journal articles that have illuminated clinical work with sexual abuse. It does not spell out specialized techniques or program models. The goal of this book is to provide a conceptual framework to guide differential diagnosis and treatment and to illustrate a developmental-contextual model.

I am indebted to the group for its commitment and spirit of openness, vulnerability, and sharing. Many times during the writing process, the members stopped short to remark that these concepts are really not so new or different. Indeed, the process has gone full circle: beginning by viewing sexual abuse as a uniquely different and devastating phenomenon of human experience, developing theories and therapies specific to the problem, eventually reaching an understanding that what is unique is the individual client, and returning to theories and therapies regarding human development and therapeutic relationships. At this writing, many colleagues around the world appear to be arriving at similar conclusions, traveling along their own roads to a new intersection.

In many ways, this text reflects what many therapists already know, but it is hoped that the reader will be able to share a sense of validation and experience renewed clarity by joining the group's process. Or perhaps the particular ways in which this group has synthesized the research and personal clinical experiences will spark some new insights beyond what is here. For younger clinicians (the new generation), the text may be a useful journey through the history behind some of the current beliefs in the field and may help to put into perspective conflicting information from different points in time.

—*Gail Ryan, M.A.*

1 Victim to Victimizer: Rethinking Victim Treatment

Gail Ryan

The potential effects of childhood sexual abuse include a wide array of dysfunctional outcomes for victims during their childhood and as adults. Victims of sexual abuse often experience emotional (Adams-Tucker, 1982), developmental (Adams-Tucker, 1980; Woodling & Kossoris, 1981), behavioral (Adams-Tucker, 1980; Woodling & Kossoris, 1981; Finkelhor, 1986; Longo, 1982; Summit, 1983), and communication problems (Blum & Gray, 1987) in childhood. They also may experience pervasive fears and feelings of helplessness (Sanford, 1987; Weiss, Rogers, Darwin, & Dutton, 1955; Longo, 1986) and depression (Woodling & Kossoris, 1981; Finkelhor, 1986; Conte, 1985b), as well as somatic complaints (Adams-Tucker, 1980; Finkelhor, 1986; Conte, 1985b). They are overrepresented in special education programs (Conte, 1985b) and in the eating disorder population as infants and adults (Haynes-Seman, 1987; Oppenheimer, Howells, Palmer, & Challoner, 1985), as well as among prostitutes (Finkelhor, 1986) and among people at risk for suicide (Adams-Tucker, 1980; Woodling & Kossoris, 1981; DeYoung, 1982), substance abuse (Evans, Schaefer, & Sterne, 1984), sexual dysfunction (Becker, Skinner, Abel, & Treacy, 1982), multiple personality (Fagan & Wexler, 1983), hysterical seizures (Goodwin, Simms, & Bergman, 1979), and other psychiatric and mental health problems (Adams-Tucker, 1982).

Reprinted with permission from the *Journal of Interpersonal Violence*, vol. 4, no. 3, September 1989, pp. 325–341.

Another negative outcome may be the increased risk of the sexually abused becoming sexually abusive to others. Studies of adult sexual offenders reveal that as many as 70 to 80 percent were sexually victimized in childhood (Groth & Longo, 1979; Longo, 1982; Kline, 1987). Many adolescents who molest children have revealed that they began such molestation by recreating their own experience of sexual abuse (Longo, 1982). Most recently, work with prepubescent victims has shown that some exhibit sexually abusive behaviors as young as age five (Cavanaugh-Johnson, 1987). This alarming outcome supports a view that sexual abuse is a learned behavior and that although not all sexually abused children become sexual offenders, they are at increased risk of developing offending behaviors (Calderone, 1983; Longo, 1986; Paperny & Deisher, 1983; Ryan, Lane, Davis, & Isaac, 1987).

> **Sexual abuse is a learned behavior, and although not all sexually abused children become sexual offenders, they are at increased risk of developing offending behaviors.**

Recognition of the many potential negative sequelae of childhood sexual abuse has motivated the demand for and creation of treatment resources for child victims of sexual abuse. This chapter hypothesizes that experience in the treatment of sexual offenders may have important implications for how we treat identified victims of child sexual abuse in order to prevent the development of sexual offending. Treatment issues present in both victims and offenders are explored, and an argument is made for rethinking current therapy methods with child sexual abuse victims.

This chapter's definitions of issues, characteristics, and manifestations of dysfunction in victims are based both on observation of male and female victims of all ages in treatment and on a review of the literature describing short- and long-term effects of sexual abuse. Direct intervention with 17 juvenile offenders, consultation with other juvenile sex offender treatment providers, and review of the descriptive literature on offenders are the bases for the hypotheses of a developmental path from victim to victimizer. The ideas set forth here are exploratory, offered in the hope of advancing the primary prevention, research, and treatment of sexual abuse by interrupting the intergenerational cycle of abuse (Haynes-Seman, 1985; Freeman-Longo, 1986).

The Experience of Abuse

The experience of sexual victimization is both the same as and different from other abusive experiences. Although sexual abuse involves emotional betrayal and psychological distress, the relationship may also meet the vulnerable child's emotional need for attention and nurturance (Summit, 1983), thus creating psychological confusion for the victim. Sexual abuse is dependent on exploitation of the victim by the offender, yet frequently the victim is the one who feels guilty and stigmatized (Conte, 1985b).

Whether the abuse is intrafamilial or extrafamilial, the victim's sense of self is endangered by the experience of being used as an object in another's schema without regard for the victim's needs or desires (Willock, 1983; Steele, 1986). The abuse may cause physical pain or injury but may also cause pleasure and/or sexual arousal. The "traumatic sexualization" (Finkelhor & Browne, 1985) may shape the child's view of sexuality in ways that are developmentally inappropriate and interpersonally dysfunctional (Conte, 1985b), and the experience may create post-traumatic stress symptoms (e.g., delusions of persecution, depression, and somatic complaints) (Adams-Tucker, 1980; Finkelhor, 1986; Sanford, 1987; Conte, 1985b). The literature on child development documents that developmental regression or arrest may occur in response to stress (Maslow, 1964). The experience of sexual abuse, therefore, may be the factor that alters development or contributes to the regressive tendencies that Groth and Birnbaum (1978) conceptualized as "fixated" or "regressive" patterns of child molesting. The traumatized child may become fixated on the trauma, recreating the experience in ritualistic patterns that become more elaborate, more rigid, and more secret over time (Terr, 1983a, 1983b). The child victim is exposed to sexual experiences in an emotional climate of fear, and the child's cognitive confusion may incorporate the offender's coercive rationalizations and distortions.

The conflicting physical and emotional sensations, psychological confusion, and feelings of intrusion may create a sense of powerlessness and lack of control that reinforce the helplessness inherent in any exploitative experience (Hiroto, 1974). The lack of control may lead to control-seeking behaviors (e.g., eating disorders, self-destruction, or exploitation of others). Female victims appear to internalize their control-seeking behaviors, whereas male victims are more likely to turn outward with aggressive and antisocial behaviors (Summit, 1983).

Also unique in sexual abuse is the climate of secrecy that isolates the child and prohibits the child from validating feelings and/or correcting distorted assumptions (Finkelhor, 1986). The child has been exposed not only to the deviant sexual experience but also to the offender's distorted thinking and rationalizations while he grooms the victim and subsequently uses coercion to protect the secret (Summit, 1983). The isolation imposed by secrecy supports the development of irrational thinking in the child, which may erode the victim's self-esteem and allow the guilt and confusion to grow without external feedback. Within such isolation, the victim feels most powerless, and anger may be translated into fantasies of retaliation in order to regain control. When fantasy becomes planning — whether consciously or unconsciously — the victim's goal is to regain the power and control that were lost in the experience of being a victim. Distorted thinking at this point may support a progression into a dysfunctional coping style, negative behavior, or criminal offending (Ryan et al., 1987). Especially for the male victim, identification with the aggressor may be more comfortable than a victim identity, whereas female victims may be more likely to show self-destructive behaviors or covert exploitation in future relationships (Summit, 1983). The traumatic experience may have a "disproportionate influence upon role taking and lead to important changes in the social self" (Kurtz, 1984, p. 171).

Treatment Issues:
Parallels in Victim and Victimizer

Simplistically, the etiology of sexual offending may be in the offender's attempt to "master" his/her own helplessness by taking the aggressor's role (Ryan, 1984). More specifically, however, we see that after the offender's experience of abuse, any subsequent situations that cause the offender to feel helpless or out of control may trigger a progression of thoughts and feelings that move the offender toward a sexual assault. The sexual assault cycle (Ryan et al., 1987) conceptualizes a situation that triggers a predictable pattern of negative feelings, cognitive distortions, and control-seeking behaviors, leading to a sexual offense. A very similar progression is seen in the dysfunctional cycle, depicted in Figure 1.1, which applies to many of the control-seeking dysfunctions.

When the young offender is first identified, poor self-image and feelings of helplessness are pervasive and often relate to some past experience of victimization or loss. Many abusers have experienced physical and/or sexual abuse, and more than half report a parental loss during early childhood (Ryan et al., 1987). In fact, the young offender's characteristics are often so victim-like that everyone can be completely deflected from the reality of the present victimization of others; the current behavior and its impact are thus minimized and denied. These offenders often perceive themselves as persecuted, helpless, and therefore not at all responsible for their behavior or their fate. In a traditional therapeutic approach, these feelings from the past would become the focus of treatment, based on the assumption that by getting in touch with the history of current problems, one comes to understand and accept oneself, and therefore the present becomes manageable.

Such history can explain sexual offending, but it must not be allowed to excuse subsequent exploitative, irresponsible, or dangerous behaviors. In order to be motivated toward significant change, one must achieve a balance between acceptance of one's history and discomfort with the present.

Sexual behavior is reinforced by a physiological reward, and as with many addictive experiences, learning theory hypothesizes a "pairing" of the stimulus and the reward (Ryan et al., 1987). When sexuality has been paired (during sexual abuse in childhood) with fear, anger, helplessness, and/or aggression, subsequent experiences of those feelings may trigger a cycle that leads to sexual arousal, reinforcing the negative pairing. Some offenders experience high arousal in response to the memory of their own abuse (Longo, 1986) and, over time, may come to use sexually aggressive fantasies and behaviors as their only coping mechanism for "feeling better." Change may require educational, behavioral, and cognitive approaches in addition to insight.

Figure 1.1 The Dysfunctional Response Cycle Experienced by Victims of Childhood Sexual Abuse

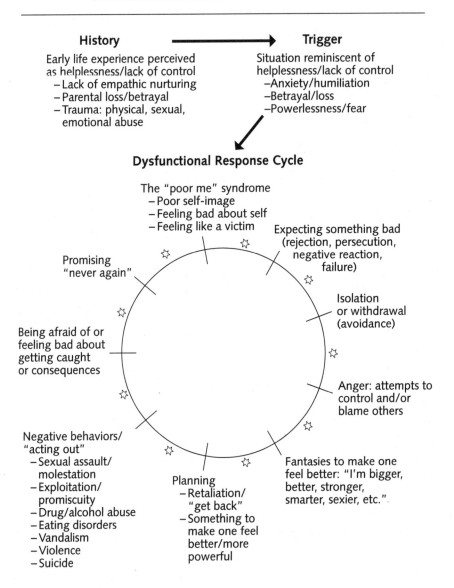

☆ = Cognitive distortions/irrational thoughts/"thinking errors" that enable progression through the cycle

For both victims and offenders, the issues of sexual abuse are those of power and control (e.g., helplessness, betrayal, humiliation, and feeling controlled). For the victim, these may be the outcome of being abused; for the offender, they become triggers for offending. These issues may be manifested in a wide variety of personality characteristics and a variety of dysfunctional behaviors (Figure 1.2). Cyclical patterns emerge as victims try to resolve their issues through negative acting out. The views outlined above lead us to draw parallels directly from the offending cycle and to identify specific issues for consideration in victim treatment.

Denial and Minimization

Sexual offenders are well known for the pervasive levels of denial and minimization that support their offending. Child victims are exposed to the perpetrator's own rationalizations and minimization and may even experience denial in people they trust when they try to disclose the abuse (Summit, 1983). Historically, victims have tried to deny their own victimization by pretending that it never happened, by blocking their memories, or by imagining that the abuse touched only their body and not their person. Children may minimize the abuse even when it becomes known, and they sometimes retract disclosures in an effort to make it not real. Male victims are especially likely to rationalize the experience by believing that they are not really victims because they are actually exploiting the abuser (Freeman-Longo, 1986).

Repression of the traumatic aspects and acceptance of the pleasurable aspects of an experience of sexual abuse may support future denial of the harmfulness of child molesting. Through denial, repression, and dissociation, the victim is defending against the effect of the abuse, but these defenses are dysfunctional because they are irrational and fail to protect victims from further abuse or dysfunctional outcomes. Irrational coping mechanisms set the stage for continued rationalizations of exploitative or dangerous

> **When parents or professionals also deny or minimize the reality of sexual abuse when it comes to light, the child's sense of reality is further confused, and the denial that supports offending is reinforced.**

Figure 1.2   Parallel Issues: Victim Outcomes/Offender Triggers

Issues	Characterized by	Manifested in
Helplessness	Poor self-image	Power/control behaviors
Powerlessness	Lack of trust	Setting-up self for failure or victimization
Lack of control	Unrealistic expectations	
Embarrassment	Expectation of rejection	Withdrawal from others
Anxiety	Expectation of failure	Putting self down
Humiliation	External locus of control	Irresponsible behaviors
Belittlement	Thinking errors/poor judgment	Property destruction
Fear	Distorted view of world	Self-destructive behaviors
Betrayal	Personalizing sexual experience	
Devaluation	Depersonalizing others	Aggression
Confusion	Deviant sexual arousal	Sexual acting out
Sexualization	Poor social interactions	Promiscuity
Isolation	Dissociative states	Sexual abuse of others
	Somatic complaints	

behaviors and interactions. When parents or professionals also deny or minimize the reality of sexual abuse when it comes to light, the child's sense of reality is further confused, and the denial that supports offending is reinforced.

Guilt and Accountability

Many times, the trigger at the beginning of the offending cycle is a situation that causes the young offender to develop the "poor me" syndrome. The tendency to feel unjustly persecuted and sorry for oneself is actually an externalization of blame and responsibility and may act as the excuse for subsequent negative outcomes. Young offenders often feel that life is unfair and that they are victims of circumstances or fate; for example, they are late "because the clock was wrong," they are out of control "because of being hyper," and they were fighting "because someone else started it." The feeling of powerlessness is so pervasive that denial of responsibility seems rational to them, and they are unable to believe in any personal connection between causes and consequences. The impact of abuse on the developing locus of control has been explored (Galambos & Dixon, 1984), and the perception of external control is pervasive in the victim/victimizer's low self-esteem and sense of powerlessness.

In the sexual offender's cycle, "transitory guilt" follows an assault; that is, the guilt is not motivated by the offending behavior or by victim empathy but is related solely to the fear or the experience of being caught, which causes the offender to "lose control" and therefore feel a failure again. Similarly, the sexually abused child's expression of guilt often has to do with the negative effects produced by disclosure rather than the sexual abuse (DeFrancis, 1969). The offender's distorted thinking is already at work: Both victim and offender believe that something bad will happen if the secret is disclosed.

In intervention with child sexual abuse victims, professionals have stressed the victims' blamelessness in trying to avoid the guilt — which is known to be devastating — by placing the responsibility for what has happened on the offender. Although this is obviously appropriate, one must also be cautious not to make the child vulnerable either to externalizing the locus of control (Hiroto, 1974) or to minimizing or denying responsibility for his/her behavior in other situations. Intervention must work toward accountability for the offender and for the victim; the child must understand that he/she must be accountable for his/her subsequent behavior, just as the offender must be accountable for his. The child must not be allowed to use the sexual abuse as an excuse for irresponsible behavior today, or he/she may continue to do so in the future.

While holding victims and offenders accountable for subsequent behavior, society also must be held accountable for protecting the child and for the failure of protection that enabled the abuse. Placing the blame with the offender may relieve the victim of guilt, but at the same time, it actually increases the victim's feeling of helplessness by defining his/her lack of control, making the child vulnerable to repeated abuse because of the "poor me, I'm a victim" attitude. When the blame is placed with the offender and the child victims are assured that they were not able to prevent the abuse, the responsibility for preventing future abuse must be placed with another adult who is as powerful in the child's mind as the offender. Children who have been sexually abused by someone who is bigger, stronger, or in a position of authority are not going to believe that anything they are taught to say or do is going to protect them from the perpetrator if they are not supported by a capable adult. Even the theory of "corrective denouement" (Terr, 1983a) requires a solution that is actually possible. Fantasy solutions based on the child outwitting or overpowering a past or potential perpetrator support the "get back" (revenge) thinking that seeks control by controlling others.

Power and Control

The sexual assault cycle manifests control-seeking behaviors. The thinking that supports the progression of fantasy and behavior reflects a frantic search for control. When expecting a negative reaction, such as rejection or failure in interpersonal transactions, the young offender takes control by either provoking or avoiding the expected. Self-isolation fulfills the expectation of aloneness, and retaliatory thinking reflects the offender's perception that he/she is a victim in an unempathic world. The subsequent fantasies are attempts to "feel better" by coming out on top in whatever scenario is imagined. Throughout the cycle, offenders first label every feeling "anger," but when the underlying cause of the anger is explored, frustration and, ultimately, helplessness are revealed. The perceived lack or loss of control triggers the cycle. The victim's experience of abuse is one of helplessness, and the most central issue for victims is the need to regain control.

"Empowerment" is a term often used in victim advocacy, but empowerment can be a two-edged sword if it is based in feelings rather than cognitions, or if it utilizes irrational hypotheses to support a false sense of control. Victims may employ irrational thinking in an effort to cope with what has occurred. By imagining that they could have prevented their abuse, they feel responsible for not having prevented the abuse rather than feeling helpless. This may be a temporarily adaptive coping mechanism that helps them feel better (Conte, 1988), but over time, it may become maladaptive as it supports the irrational thinking that holds victims rather than offenders accountable. The victim who thinks that he/she could have prevented the abuse "if only I had screamed" may become the offender who believes that victims wanted the sexual abuse because "they didn't scream."

True empowerment cannot be located externally or in fantasy. It must come from within one's own sense of self-esteem and be based in rational thought if it is to be real and functional. True empowerment is the ability to examine one's thinking and correct the erroneous assumptions that control the emotional and psychological impact of one's experiences. Through rational thinking, the victim regains control — not by controlling others, but by controlling the impact others have on him/her. The limits of power in childhood must be recognized: often, children cannot control situations, and they should not be encouraged to try to control others. The child's power is in self-control, strength discovery, and the ability to identify and rely on supportive, protective adults.

Anger and Retaliation

One of the strongest feelings in response to betrayal and helplessness is anger. Traditionally, therapists try to help clients uncover anger — feel it, label it, work through it. Displays of anger and even violent behavior within the "safe" environment of play therapy have been allowed and even encouraged in the belief that acting out the anger resolves it and lifts the victim out of helplessness (Mann & McDermott, 1983). The cathartic effect has been assumed. Research findings, however, demonstrate that a cathartic effect cannot be assumed in relation to aggression. Acting out may actually reinforce rather than reduce aggression (Goldstein, 1987).

In therapy with child victims, Terr, in her work with "post-traumatic play," has demonstrated that for the traumatized child, "reenactment does not work to dissipate anxiety" (Terr, 1983b, p. 314). The child was not protected or rescued from the traumatic experience and therefore may not believe in heroes or any powerful goodness. Because the power of the trauma continues, the child's sense of control depends on preserving a known that can be anticipated rather than venturing into an uncontrollable unknown. Because the child's play deals with actual external events, the experience cannot always be reworked through play. Terr describes trauma reenacted in play as becoming solidified rather than resolved (Terr, 1983b).

In the young offender's cycle, anger and retaliation behaviors support the progression toward a sexual assault, and therapy works to back away, analyze the thinking, and resolve the anger cognitively rather than emotionally or behaviorally. Learning to "rethink" situations to reduce negative feelings is stressed rather than "acting out" the negative feelings. For the young offender, aggressive acting out — especially sexually aggressive thoughts and behaviors — supports and reinforces rather than reduces the risk of victimizing others. For these offenders, acting out signals a grave danger of reoffending.

It is interesting to note that child sexual abuse victims aged 6 to 12 demonstrate higher incidents of psychopathology and externalized symptoms (aggressive, antisocial, and undercontrolled behaviors) than either younger or older victims (Friedrich, Urquiza, & Beilke, 1986). Many teenage offenders report first practicing offender behavior and experiencing offender thinking during that same age span (6 to 12 years old).

In one clinical setting, male sexual abuse victims aged 6 to 11 were already demonstrating offending patterns that were far from being situational, "sexually reactive" incidents when evaluated for victim treatment. These young victim/victimizers were planning, calculating, and rationalizing in the same way that older offenders do as they picked and groomed potential victims and carried out the abuse (Isaac, 1987).

It has been assumed that acting out in play is imaginary and/or cathartic. A preliminary study of serious juvenile sexual offenders supports the fear that catharsis is not produced by sexual aggression in play. In structured interviews using open-ended questions about memories of childhood play, Law (1987) interviewed 12 incarcerated adolescent sexual offenders who were participating in an offense-specific treatment group. Twenty-five percent of the study sample described sexually aggressive scenarios with stuffed animals in early childhood, and an additional 25 percent reported cruelty to animals in latency. As juvenile offenders in treatment, they recalled these behaviors as "practicing" their sexual assaults. The behaviors reported with the stuffed animals included mutilation, urination, and penetration, as well as physical and verbal aggression. The fantasies they reported included the same calculating and coercive thinking that later supported their exploitation of children. One juvenile recounted conversations with his "teddy" wherein the teddy's refusal to comply in sexually abusive scenes triggered the teddy's complete destruction (Law, 1987).

Diagnostically, the victim's anger and the desire to retaliate must be identified, but professionals may need to rethink the resolution so that the intervention does not inadvertently reinforce distorted thinking or negative behavior and thus support the prognosis of subsequent dysfunction. Victims often show increased acceptance of aggressive behaviors and expectations for retribution (Kurtz, 1984). Child victims who are acting out aggression are already in touch with their anger and should not be encouraged to act out retaliation scenarios or sexually abusive experiences. Accountability must be introduced in therapy. Cognitive resolution can be supported by aversive imagery that pairs negative consequences with exploitative behaviors, and victim empathy should be stressed. The therapist's role should be to discover nonaggressive resolution and attach the reality of negative outcomes to aggression.

> **Child victims who are acting out aggression are already in touch with their anger and should not be encouraged to act out retaliation scenarios or sexually abusive experiences. Accountability must be introduced in therapy.**

"Retaliation thinking" in parents and professionals who respond to the child's disclosure reinforces dysfunctional thinking for the child. Intervention should include evaluating the family's initial reactions and ongoing coping in order to be aware of well-meaning but destructive models. Parents sometimes feel personally violated by the molestation of their child and may openly manifest both power/control behaviors and retaliation plans. A distinction must be made between accountability and retaliation, and irrational solutions should be countered.

Fantasies and Reinforcement

The fantasies that young offenders engage in to imagine feeling better are the step between the anger at their powerlessness and the planning of their sexual assault. The content of fantasy may be positive or negative, and it both reflects and reinforces as role play the strengths or weaknesses of the individual's thinking. When a fantasy based on distorted or deviant thinking is not subject to external reaction, correction, or validation, it may reinforce deviant thoughts and actually lead to execution of what was imagined. In other cases, irrational or distorted thinking may enable the offender to act out an appropriate fantasy with an inappropriate partner. Fantasies may be based in past experience; when that experience was sexual abuse, the fantasy may reinforce the pleasurable physical sensations (especially when paired with masturbation) and suppress the negative consequences. Signs of selective suppression ("It wasn't so bad" or "I deserved it") may reflect thinking errors that support offending.

In play therapy, children who cannot verbalize their thinking are often allowed to play out their fantasies, feelings, and experiences. Although the therapist should respond to the content of their play by accepting their feelings, the therapist should carefully separate that acceptance from the negative behaviors and work to bring conflict resolution into a cognitive framework. Adults must recognize that children look to them for verification, correction, and teaching.

While accepting the validity of the child's negative feelings about the abusive experience, therapists must be willing to confront irrational perceptions and offer rational alternatives. Behavioral expressions of aggression should be carefully limited to a period of diagnosis; accountability for and consequences of behaviors that demonstrate irrational thinking and victimize others should quickly be introduced. Fantasy thinking and play should be carefully monitored for demonstrations of power and control that victimize others, and more appropriate means of exercising power should be introduced. The child who personalizes the punching bag or names the doll and then destroys it should be redirected into more functional and empathic anger management. Scenarios of anger and retaliation are role plays for aggression and victimization; they should be minimized and countered rather than encouraged or allowed.

Secrets and Confidentiality

Sexual abuse occurs in secret, and secrecy enables it to continue. In juvenile sex offender treatment, most providers require a waiver of confidentiality in a clear statement that the offender must be willing to give up the secrecy that has supported his/her offending. Victim treatment providers may need to rethink the traditional role of confidentiality in therapy in order to help the victim give up secrecy as well.

The secrets of sexual abuse have been established by the offender through coercion and/or threats, and the victim's perception of the power of the secret must be understood. The child's fear of full disclosure may be based on the expectation of a negative reaction (e.g., "my parent may not love me" or "people will think I am a bad person" if the whole secret is known) or on the continuing perception of the offender being more powerful than any other available protector. As long as the secret remains isolated from the child's world, it may continue to be powerful.

If the child succeeds in full disclosure to those whom he/she was warned not to tell and experiences a supportive reaction rather than the feared trouble, the secret is dispelled and loses its power. Legitimate privacy and dangerous secrecy must be distinguished, and the victim's full disclosure of the abuse must be supported. If the secrets of abuse are kept in the therapeutic relationship, the therapy may inadvertently support the problems of denial, minimization, and vulnerability.

Empathy

Victim empathy is a key element in the prevention of sexual abuse, and therapists must be aware that many child victims were vulnerable to the perpetrator's advances because they had never experienced empathy (Willock, 1983; Isaac, 1987). For the child who has not experienced consistent empathic care in early childhood, the nurturance offered by the offender during the "grooming" stage and whatever pleasure the child may experience in the relationship may be viewed as a fair trade against the negative aspects of the abusive experience (Isaac, 1987) — a point of view supported by the offender's own statements. The child is at high risk of identifying with the aggressor, incorporating the offender's distorted thinking patterns. The child inevitably uses a mode of interpretation reflective of earlier life as he or she tries to cope with this severe test of his or her sense of self and of personal worth. The therapist must try to step into the child's frame of reference and truly understand his/her experience of the abuse in order to counter the erroneous assumptions the child has attached to the exploitative relationship. It cannot be assumed that every child's experience of abuse is the same. The victim's own pain must be identified and experienced if he/she is to understand the pain of others; the capacity for empathy must begin within oneself.

Rethinking Victim Treatment

When appropriate interventions for sexual abuse victims are being considered, prior knowledge and existing modalities should not be disregarded, but the therapist's role should be rethought in light of the unique experience of sexual abuse. Interventions should be designed specifically to address and restructure those thoughts and feelings that may lead to dysfunctional behaviors such as sexual offending.

The dysfunctional cycle (Figure 1.1) conceptualizes the way in which situations, thoughts, feelings, and behaviors may interact to lead to a negative outcome for victims. The cycle is triggered by situations reminiscent of earlier trauma, which recreate similar feelings of helplessness, lack of control, and loss of trust. On the basis of negative past experiences, the expectation that other bad things will happen — especially in interpersonal relationships — begins movement into the cycle. Loss of trust prevents confidence in approaching new relationships and supports fear of rejection, persecution, and betrayal. Rather than risk new failures, an individual may seek control over interpersonal relationships either by avoiding them (i.e., withdrawing from the situation) or by controlling the rejection (i.e., behaving in ways that guarantee a negative reaction), resulting in self-isolation.

In this period of isolation, anger leads to "power and control" behaviors designed to blame or control others, and to fantasies of solutions that might feel better. In these fantasies, what was lost in the past is regained, and retaliation is effected. This "get back" thinking is symptomatic and dysfunctional because it imagines that past trauma can actually be undone. When the fantasies become plans, the individual seeks control, either personally in order to achieve internal control (e.g., through eating disorders, substance abuse, or suicide) or interpersonally in order to achieve external control (e.g., through property destruction, violence, exploitation, promiscuity, or sexual assault). The negative behavior is temporarily empowering but fails to achieve permanent gain in self-esteem because the fear of discovery and the reality of negative consequences recall the original lack of control and the individual's feelings of powerlessness. This cycle is evident in the coping styles of some victims and should be specifically addressed.

Just as juvenile sex offender therapy has evolved into an eclectic modality utilizing a combination of cognitive, educational, behavioral, and psychodynamic approaches, victim treatment may need an eclectic model to address the same issues. If the ultimate goal of victim treatment is to prevent dysfunctional outcomes, exploitative behaviors, and irrational, unempathic thinking, the therapist must confront inappropriate behaviors, counter irrational interpretations of life experiences, and restructure exploitative thinking. Directive, educational, and cognitive approaches may be needed to counter cognitive distortions, whereas the therapist's empathy counters the depersonalization of sexual abuse.

Many behavior modification approaches widely used in residential child care facilities are inherently manipulable and may support rather than diminish the power and control issues of abuse victims. The child's ability to calculate and exploit such systems and receive predictable negative or positive consequences may foster in the child exploitative thinking and rationalizations that reinforce the manipulative use of power and control for self-gratification. Immediate behavior management is necessary, but long-term dysfunctions must be considered as well. It is only by monitoring the cognitive perceptions of the child that exploitative thinking can be separated from the facade of compliance and/or failure.

> **It is only by monitoring the cognitive perceptions of the child that exploitative thinking can be separated from the façade of compliance and/or failure.**

Groth and Birnbaum's (1978) conceptualization of adult molesters as being either "fixated" or "regressed" supports a hypothesis that offending patterns may have been established in an earlier developmental stage and either have become the primary mode of sexual gratification or are regressed to in times of stress. Evidence of developmental repression in sexually abused children (Woodling & Kossoris, 1981) supports the application of the same hypothesis in victim treatment. Therapists can use such information to address the early appearances of offending and, by holding the child victim accountable for responsible behavior and rational thought, to prevent reinforcement of offending patterns.

This chapter has suggested that traditional therapy approaches alone may not be adequate to prevent the development of offending behaviors in child sexual abuse victims. The suggestion is based on the parallels in victim and offender treatment issues, offender histories that demonstrate the development of sexually abusive behaviors, and the knowledge that traditional insight-oriented therapy alone is not successful in changing sexually offending behaviors. Patterns of denial and minimization, power and control behaviors, irrational thinking, irresponsible decision making, retaliation fantasies, deviant sexual arousal, aggression, secrecy, and preoccupation with or reenactment of one's own victimization are areas of concern that may warrant special consideration and specific interventions in relation to the sexual assault cycle.

Although controlled studies are needed to test these hypotheses, the implications of offender treatment discussed here should be cause enough to reexamine the use of traditional practices alone in the treatment of child victims of sexual abuse. The testimony of adolescent offenders as well as the recognition of sexually offending behaviors developing in prepubescent children can surely teach us something about prevention of and early intervention in these behaviors.

2

Developing a Contextual Matrix

Gail Ryan and Associates

Carol Bilbrey, John Dick, Tim Fuente, Candace Grosz, Carol Haase, Phil Hyden, Connie Isaac, Ruth Kempe, Sandy Lane, Jeff Metzner, Courtney Pullen, Emili Rambus, Lindsay March Schweitzer, Brandt Steele, Bob Wagstaff, Sherri Wand, and Jerry Yager

I n the mid-1980s, many clinicians and researchers were hypothesizing that differential outcomes for victims of sexual abuse would
be related to various combinations of factors associated with the
experience of the abuse and/or the process of discovery or disclosure. As the research became available, the study group reviewed
papers and articles detailing the data related to various aspects of
these experiences and the subsequent outcomes of individuals. This
review of the literature spanned the work of colleagues studying victims, perpetrators, and survivors, as well as studies of the various disorders reporting disproportionate numbers of clients with childhood
sexual abuse in their histories.

Many of these studies were born out of common sense: com-
paring more coercive, intrusive, and long-term abuse experiences
with less threatening, less intrusive, and more isolated incidents. Age
was considered as a variable as well, with some researchers hypothesizing that sexualization and intrusion earlier in childhood might
correlate to important differences.

Although many researchers confirmed that such variables
seemed to account for some of the differences in subsequent outcomes, the correlations were inadequate to provide a convincing

Special thanks to Debra Grove and Scott Plejdrup for their contributions to the discussions on which this chapter is based.

explanation of a causal effect. Although some survivors with better outcomes did come from the "older/less intrusive" groups and some with more pervasive dysfunction came from the "younger/more intrusive" groups, there were many exceptions to the trend. There were many reports of survivors doing very well (exhibiting little or no impairment in relationships and functioning) despite severe, long-term abuse at very young ages or even for many years throughout childhood and adolescence. At the same time, there were many reports of extreme impairment among individuals with single incidents of abuse and/or histories of less intrusive, short-term abuse experiences.

Similarly, some researchers were hypothesizing that variables in the nature of the relationship between the child victim and the abuser might be relevant (e.g., familial versus extrafamilial or parent versus extended family or sibling). However, these correlations also did not demonstrate a definitive causal pathway to the outcomes. Despite a wealth of clinical and methodological data, no single variable or constellation of descriptors adequately explained dysfunctional outcomes.

There were also a number of studies exploring variables associated with the disclosure of the abuse. Many hypothesized that the child who told right away, was believed, and was effectively protected would experience less impairment than the child who was either unable to tell or not believed (and consequently not protected). Again, correlations were often significant but still not convincing.

Returning to the hypothesis of the victim becoming victimizer (see Chapter 1), the group pondered the distinctions between the underlying issues, the ways in which those issues became "characterized" in the individual, and the behavioral manifestations or "symptoms." Believing in the connection between the victim issues and the compensatory function of the cycle, the group relied heavily on clinical experiences to explore the pathway through subsequent life experience to try to understand what might be moderating or exacerbating the risks.

By this time, the piles of literature and notes were becoming unmanageable. In an attempt to contain and organize all this information, descriptors of variables were separated into categories, and a matrix began to develop (Figure 2.1). Just laying all these variables out in a systematic fashion impressed on the group the complexity of the question, as well as the uniqueness of each victim's experiential path.

The group continued to believe that the dysfunctional cycle represented a particular model or style of coping that became the vehicle of the compensatory disorders. A new series of questions began to be articulated. If the cycle represents a common defensive strategy for individuals experiencing a sense of vulnerability and seeking a sense of control, then:

1. Which victims are most likely to rely on external sources to achieve that sense of control?

2. What influences the type of behavior the individual imagines will provide that sense of control?

3. What influences whether the individual acts on the fantasized solution?

4. What causes the initial "acting out" to become habitual?

The group reviewed numerous theories and studies related to coping, resilience, accommodation, habituation, and locus of control. At the same time, the group was delving into the literature describing diagnostic and clinical work related to each of the compensatory dysfunction categories. Many of the disorders of interest were treated in specialized treatment programs and were the basis of specific research studies (e.g., eating disorders, substance abuse, sexual addictions, self-destructive behavior, depression, sexual offending, violence). Practitioners of these various subspecialties were learning a great deal about these different disorders. However, it became noteworthy that there were many areas of overlap among both the clients and the issues.

During the time the group was studying the dysfunctional outcomes, the survivor movement was gaining momentum. More data were becoming available, continuing to indicate that although many survivors experienced long-term difficulties, many others had done very well despite their not having had treatment as children. It became apparent that it was not *only* a history of victimization but more likely some combination of victimization and other factors that increased the risk of compensatory behavioral disorders.

The group focused for a time on the cycle — exploring the client's selection of fantasy material and appreciating that the function of fantasy in the cycle was to answer the individual's questions:

Figure 2.1 Experience of Sexual Abuse

EXPERIENCE OF SEXUAL ABUSE

| Sexual humiliation or trauma | Hands off: peep, flash, obscenity | Observation: nudity, sexual abuse of other; pornography: literature, photo, video; uncomprehendable sexual stimuli | Hands on: fondling, genital stimulation, frottage | Penetration: oral, vaginal, anal; digital, penile, objectile | Genital injury |

Age/Developmental Stage

Relationship of abuser:	Stranger	Peer	Adolescent	Sibling	Known adult	Caretaker	Parent
Child's perception of relationship:	Roles/expectations			Casual/authority/dependency		Trust/distrust	
Duration:	Onetime		Repetitive			Chronic	
Method of engagement:	Seduction	Trickery	Bribes, lures	Coercion	Threat of loss	Threat of force	Force	Violence

Child's perception:	Cognitive: Understanding of offender's distortions	Physical: pain, arousal, comfort	Emotional: fear, anxiety, pleasure	Secondary gains or motive

DISCLOSURE

Consequences of disclosure:	Expedient	Delayed	Nondisclosure
	Effective intervention	Ineffective intervention	No intervention

Victim: fear, shame, guilt, blame, placement, loss of family, not believed — abuse continues

Family: rage, confusion, intrusion, breakup, loss of members, denial/minimalization

Offender: deny or admit, legal threats, personal threats, suicide, loss

Figure 2.1 Experience of Sexual Abuse (cont.)

OUTCOMES

Issues:
anxiety; humiliation; lack of control; helplessness, vulnerability, powerlessness; embarrassment, shame, guilt; put down, betrayed, devalued; post-traumatic stress; loss; confusion: sexual, cognitive, role, boundary, relationship

Characteristics:
poor self image, lack of trust, distorted thinking, negative expectations; rejection, failure, personalizing sexual offense, depersonalizing others, preoccupation, depression, fear of intimacy, sadness, deviant sexual arousal, indiscriminate external locus of control

Manifestations:
setting self up, power/control behaviors, phobias, withdrawal, isolating, post-traumatic stress disorder, unrealistic expectations, irresponsible behaviors, thinking errors, putting self down, somatic complaints, attention deficit, learning disability, promiscuity, aggression, self-destructive behavior, sexual acting out, sexual abuse perpetration/revictimization

Subsequent Life Experience

LONG-TERM OUTCOMES

Nonsexual dysfunctions:
eating disorders, substance abuse, depression, vandalism, aggression/violence, suicide, psychosis

Sexual Dysfunctions

Hypersexual:
promiscuity, sexual addiction, compulsive masturbation

Sexual offending:
rape, child molestation, exhibitionism, voyeurism, frottage, etc.

Hyposexual:
inhibited desire or arousal aversion, frigid, impotent

5% Psychotic

65–70% Paraphilia (sexual deviance)

20–30% Antisocial (other criminal behavior)

No long-term dysfunction

(1) What will make me feel better? (compensation); (2) How can I get back a sense of control? (control seeking); (3) How can I share these bad feelings in order to express my own experience or dilute the effects (validation); and (4) How can I get back at those who are perceived to be the source of my vulnerability? (retaliation). The plan to act on the fantasy is influenced by the individual's repertoire of imagined "solutions" that might address those questions, and the decision to act out the imagined solution is dependent on the access and opportunity to do so, combined with the conditions that Finkelhor (1986) described as the ability to overcome inhibitions that would ordinarily dissuade an individual from engaging in a harmful, deviant, or taboo behavior. Access and opportunity are situational variables (not always within the individual's control).

For example, one might imagine that drugs or alcohol would solve the need for compensation; but if such substances cannot be obtained, the fantasy cannot be acted on. Similarly, if the imagined control involves controlling other persons, skills and competency may be deficient to effectively act out the fantasy, or thoughts of retaliation against some aggressor may be turned against some less threatening or more available object (vandalism, violence, abusive behavior) or against oneself (self-destructive behaviors).

The answer to the question of habituation seemed apparent: behaviors that provided a temporary sense of control, especially when paired with a physiological reinforcement (such as food, alcohol, drugs, sexual satisfaction, or tension reduction), were likely to be repeated. Depressed or suicidal outcomes also seemed reinforcing in managing the overwhelming emotions that some individuals describe related to the "triggers" or the fear or the rage. Yet understanding the logic of the dysfunctional compensatory solution did not explain the negative expectations and hopelessness that seemed to fuel the cycle and perpetuate the individual's tendency to continue to reexperience the sense of helplessness described as a "victim stance."

The sense of competence versus helplessness seemed relevant to differential outcomes. Indeed, many clinicians were approaching the issue of "learned helplessness" by positing that "mastery" might hold the key to better outcomes. Unfortunately, many of the interventions being suggested as "empowering" victims to overcome the victim stance involve either irrational cognitive solutions (e.g., a 5-year-old believing that she could stop further victimization by overpowering a potential perpetrator) or control-seeking aggression dependent on external outlets (such as pounding pillows or acting out retaliatory aggression in play). The group questioned the long-term efficacy of such solutions, especially in light of an emerging body of literature suggesting that aggression was not effectively diminished by "catharsis" of anger (e.g., see Goldstein, 1987). Goldstein's work seemed to support the group's hypothesis that many of the empowering techniques suggested in victim treatment manuals might actually constitute the same temporary solutions reflected in the dysfunctional cycle.

In studying control-seeking behaviors and functional survival, locus of control and resilience issues pointed to developmental competencies. Summit's article "The Child Sexual Abuse Accommodation Syndrome" (1983) eloquently illuminated the child victim's struggle to manage and make sense of his or her experience of abuse and the subsequent consequences. "Accommodation" is described in the developmental literature as a process that relates to perceptual variables, that is, the dissonance or congruence of the abuse experience in relation to the child's prior life experience. The group hypothesized that the repertoire of potential choices of cognitive meaning, coping styles, and compensatory behaviors might be learned from the child's role models, and outcomes might be more related to variables in the child's experience before the abuse than to any particular descriptors of the abuse itself.

As the focus shifted to the developmental, cognitive, and perceptual variables, the group turned its attention to the phenomenology of the child (the child's view of the world). Taking the child's perspective meant putting aside adult assumptions about childhood victimization and appreciating that the child's experience of the abuse is the product of perceptions, beliefs, and meanings that the *child* attributes to the event. Each child's experience of sexually abusive interactions is unique because each child is unique. The options available for understanding and managing the experience are uniquely personal as well.

With a renewed respect for the complexity of the original question, the group began to hypothesize which variables in the child, the family, and the prior life experience might be most relevant and influential in shaping how the child perceives and accommodates the experience of sexual abuse in the *context* of his/her view of the world (Figure 2.2). Many of these variables were drawn from the experiences of clinicians treating adolescents and adults, looking retrospectively at risk factors and protective factors. During this course of study, the findings of Prentky et al. (1989) regarding the significance of parental loss, inconsistent care, and sexual deviance in the family of origin of adult sexual abuse perpetrators paralleled findings in the data being collected by the National Adolescent Perpetrator Network (Ryan et al., 1996), which also described a high incidence of parental loss, disrupted relationships, and dysfunctional family systems.

In her search for factors that related to the victim-victimizer progression, Gilgun (1988) described early life factors that seemed to "block" abusive outcomes and were developmental in nature. For example, the importance of having some confidant during childhood is related to basic trust, and the sexual environment in the home is clearly relevant to the child's accommodation to the sexual aspects of an abuse experience.

With these final additions, the matrix was complete (Figure 2.3) and became a map on which to plot different developmental pathways that traverse (rather than begin with) the experience of sexual abuse. The implications of such a contextual view are enormous and support a more personal and holistic approach to child victims. Although victims may share common issues, the ways in which they manage and interpret those issues *cannot be assumed*. Clinicians must put aside personal bias and be open to explore the meaning of sexual victimization in the context of the client's life experience.

A panel of study group members presented the matrix to colleagues at the Kempe Center's 18th annual Child Abuse and Neglect Symposium in 1989, along with a plea for more personalized treatment based on the unique developmental-contextual realities of clients. While supporting the efficacy of structured psychoeducational groups that address the issues victims seem to have in common, the group suggested that treatment must also validate the unique experience and perception of the individual, explore the options available in the individual's repertoire of coping strategies, and provide a new experience in the therapeutic relationship. The matrix became a guide to the complexity of the human experience of childhood sexual abuse.

Figure 2.2 Early Life Experience

	Temperament		Physical			Neurological
CONDITION AT BIRTH — endowment, family of origin	**Parental expectations:** Sex of child, Appearance, Temperament, Behavior	**Coping styles:** Communication, Problem solving, Adaptation	**Characteristics:** Enmeshed/disengaged, Rigid/chaotic, Role reversals/boundaries	**Defense mechanisms:** Distortion, Denial/avoidance, Rationalization		**Environment:** Parental violence, Support systems, Economic stress, Sexual attitudes, Intimacy
HISTORY — early childhood experience prior to sexual abuse	**Empathic care:** Trust, Confident	**Neglectful care:** Emotional, Environmental, Consistency	**Learning styles:** Disability, Opportunity	**Physical abuse:** Acute, Chronic	**Emotional abuse:** Attack, Confusion	**Substance-abusing parents**	**Parental loss:** Illness, Depression, Divorce, Death, Out-of-home placement, Sibling loss	**Rejection:** Betrayal, Abandonment	**Trauma**

Figure 2.3 Contextual Matrix: Sexual Abuse in the Context of Whole Life Experience

	Temperament	Physical		Neurological
CONDITION AT BIRTH (endowment, family of origin)	**Parental expectations:** Sex of child, Appearance, Temperament, Behavior	**Coping styles:** Communication, Problem solving, Adaptation · **Characteristics:** Enmeshed/disengaged, Rigid/chaotic, Role reversals/boundaries	**Defense mechanisms:** Distortion, Denial/avoidance, Rationalization	**Environment:** Parental violence, Support systems, Economic stress, Sexual attitudes, Intimacy
HISTORY (early childhood experience prior to sexual abuse)	**Empathic care:** Trust, Confident	**Neglectful care:** Emotional, Environmental, Consistency · **Learning styles:** Disability, Opportunity · **Physical abuse:** Acute, Chronic · **Emotional abuse:** Attack, Confusion · **Substance-abusing parents** · **Parental loss:** Illness, Depression, Divorce, Death, Out-of-home placement, Sibling loss		**Rejection:** Betrayal, Abandonment · **Trauma**

EXPERIENCE OF SEXUAL ABUSE

Sexual humiliation or trauma — Hands off: peep, flash, obscenity — Observation: nudity, sexual abuse of other; pornography: literature, photo, video; uncomprehendable sexual stimuli — Hands on: fondling, genital stimulation, frottage — Penetration: oral, vaginal, anal; digital, penile, objectile — Genital injury

Age/Developmental Stage

Relationship of abuser:	Stranger	Peer	Adolescent	Sibling	Known adult	Caretaker	Parent
Child's perception of relationship:		Roles/expectations		Casual/authority/dependency		Trust/distrust	
Duration:			Onetime		Repetitive		Chronic
Method of engagement:	Seduction	Trickery	Bribes, lures	Coercion	Threat of loss	Threat of force	Force	Violence

Child's perception: Cognitive: Understanding of offender's distortions — Physical: pain, arousal, comfort — Emotional: fear, anxiety, pleasure — Secondary gains or motive

	Expedient	Delayed	Nondisclosure
	Effective intervention	Ineffective intervention	No intervention

DISCLOSURE

Consequences of disclosure:

Victim: fear, shame, guilt, blame, placement, loss of family, not believed — abuse continues

Family: rage, confusion, intrusion, breakup, loss of members, denial/minimalization

Offender: deny or admit, legal threats, personal threats, suicide, loss

OUTCOMES

Issues: anxiety; humiliation; lack of control; helplessness, vulnerability, powerlessness; embarrassment, shame, guilt; put down, betrayed, devalued; post-traumatic stress; loss; confusion: sexual, cognitive, role, boundary, relationship

Characteristics: poor self image, lack of trust, distorted thinking, negative expectations; rejection, failure, personalizing sexual offense, depersonalizing others, preoccupation, depression, fear of intimacy, sadness, deviant sexual arousal, indiscriminate external locus of control

Manifestations: setting self up, power/control behaviors, phobias, withdrawal, isolating, post-traumatic stress disorder, unrealistic expectations, irresponsible behaviors, thinking errors, putting self down, somatic complaints, attention deficit, learning disability, promiscuity, aggression, self-destructive behavior, sexual acting out, sexual abuse perpetration/revictimization

LONG-TERM OUTCOMES

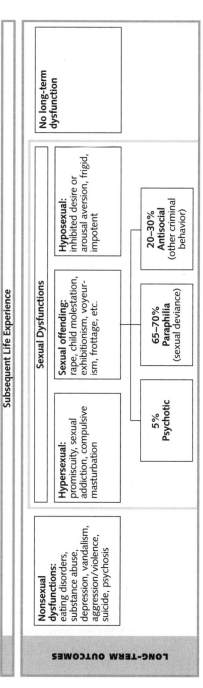

Subsequent Life Experience

Nonsexual dysfunctions: eating disorders, substance abuse, depression, vandalism, aggression/violence, suicide, psychosis

Sexual Dysfunctions

Hypersexual: promiscuity, sexual addiction, compulsive masturbation

Sexual offending: rape, child molestation, exhibitionism, voyeurism, frottage, etc.

Hyposexual: inhibited desire or arousal aversion, frigid, impotent

- 5% Psychotic
- 65–70% Paraphilia (sexual deviance)
- 20–30% Antisocial (other criminal behavior)

No long-term dysfunction

New papers and presentations by colleagues around the world have continued to illuminate, enrich, challenge, and validate the work. A few landmarks along the way stand out.

Shortly after the group's first presentation of the matrix, Hindman's book *Just Before Dawn* (1989) described a course of study that reached similar conclusions regarding the role of victim *perceptions* in predicting outcomes. Hindman's conclusions regarding the uniqueness of individual experience paralleled and validated the group's work. She describes a series of perceptual variables that cannot be gleaned from the records but can be discovered only by therapists' willingness to hear from clients about their unique experiences.

The group was also influenced by one member's casual articulation of the obvious: that every client's life experience is affected by the equally complex matrices of the people around him/her (especially those of family members) and eventually by the therapist's matrix as well. A new level of exploration and honesty required the group to appreciate what each interventionist brings to his or her relationship with the client. In addition, since this observation came from a pediatrician, it brought a new appreciation of the many variables contributed to the child's perception of the abuse experience by the multidisciplinary professionals involved in investigation and diagnostic procedures.

> In every client's life experience, he or she was also affected by the equally complex matrices of the surrounding people (especially those of family members) and eventually by the therapist's matrix as well.

The group was also influenced by the emerging body of research on and understanding of post-traumatic stress. Regarding childhood post-traumatic stress disorder (PTSD), the works of Terr (such as *Too Scared to Cry*, 1990b) spoke of the "ritualization" of post-traumatic play, a reference that increased the group's understanding of the inefficiency of play therapy in changing some behavioral symptoms. The work of van der Kolk and his colleagues (*Psychological Trauma*, 1987) examined and illuminated neurological and experiential outcomes of trauma victims and added a new appreciation that the neurological functioning that affects chemical secretions in the brain in response to stress may be permanently altered by experiences of traumatic abuse. Spiegel and colleagues (1993) further stimulated the group's application of PTSD research by describing treatment processes that were congruent with many of the group's earlier conclusions (specifically, "The Eight C's of Traumatic Dissociation Therapy").

Throughout the years, the group continued to be concerned that much of what was written regarding the actual treatment of clients relevant to sexual abuse problems described cognitive and behavioral techniques with little meaningful reference to developmental and contextual factors and even less attention to the therapeutic relationship. This was especially apparent in the literature relevant to treatment of perpetrators, young children, and addictive disorders. Yet when group members spoke with colleagues about their programs and clients, it was apparent that much more was happening in therapy than was being described in the literature. Most colleagues described their programs in sterile and didactic terms, yet case examples often revealed an underlying understanding that each client was unique. Still, there seemed to be a tremendous temptation for therapists to look for a "recipe" that could be applied to all clients without going through the painful and time-consuming process of eliciting the life experience and phenomenology of each client. This tendency seemed partly related to the toll that such in-depth work takes from therapists and is exacerbated by resource-related pressures to provide short-term therapies.

The group's more recent work has been to articulate the implications of the matrix in clinical practice by exploring its relationship to developmental theories and to describe a therapeutic relationship that is guided by and responsive to the client's unique phenomenology and will influence the context of subsequent life experience in ways that moderate the long-term risks.

3

Attachment, Separation, and Abuse Outcomes: Influence of Early Life Experience and the Family of Origin

Barry R. Lindstrom

A s Discussed in Chapter 2, attempts to rely on individual variables related to the child, the perpetrator, or the nature of an abuse experience fail to adequately explain the differential outcomes of childhood sexual abuse. Having arrived at the hypothesis that it may be the child's perception of the abuse, and the meanings attributed to it, that are most influential, the child's view of self and of the world becomes a critical element in accounting for differential outcomes.

The group hypothesized that from a developmental perspective, the quality of the child's early attachments would be a primary determinant of the developing sense of self and others. The internalization (or internal representation) of primary attachment relationships becomes the basis for the child's unique view of the world and understanding of later life experiences and relationships — including the experience of sexual victimization. Therefore, variables that might affect the quality of attachment relationships in the first few years of life and the coping styles evident in the child's role models seemed particularly relevant. These variables are contained within the first three levels of the matrix (see Figure 3.1).

Special thanks to Brandt Steele, M.D., for his comments on an earlier draft of this chapter.

Attachment is the result of an interaction among what the child brings to his/her earliest relationships (endowment), what the caregivers bring to these relationships (family of origin), and the quality of subsequent experiences (early childhood experience). Each of these factors influences and is influenced by the child's attempts to master the developmental tasks of infancy and early childhood, including the development of basic trust, personal competence, and autonomy (Erikson, 1959). The child's negotiation of these early developmental steps is likely to influence the ability to cope with subsequent life experiences or traumas. In particular, the child's perception of the abuse as congruent or dystonic with his/her former view of self and of the world and the models of coping available to the child appear to be critical issues in the treatment process and outcomes.

Although no single variable can be isolated as causative for long-term outcomes, the matrix identifies the variables that seem most relevant. Each variable on the matrix contributes multiple potentials to the individual's experience, perception, and ability to cope when abuse occurs. Although a child's primary attachment relationships establish the internalized model for subsequent interactions, other factors also influence individual developmental pathways. From the field of developmental psychopathology — with a transactional emphasis on the parent-child relationship as a precursor to later adaptation or malfunction — comes the concept of potentiating and compensating factors that either exacerbate or mitigate the effects of variables within the child's developmental pathway. This transactional model has been applied to many factors, including child maltreatment (Cicchetti, 1987) and maternal depression (Cummings & Cicchetti, 1990). The matrix suggests that this model also can be applied to understanding the outcomes of child sexual abuse.

> **Each variable on the matrix contributes multiple potentials to the individual's experience, perception, and ability to cope when abuse occurs.**

Figure 3.1 Early Life Experience

	Temperament	Physical	Neurological

CONDITION AT BIRTH — endowment / family of origin

Temperament		Physical		Neurological
Parental expectations: Sex of child, Appearance, Temperament, Behavior	**Coping styles:** Communication, Problem solving, Adaptation	**Characteristics:** Enmeshed/disengaged, Rigid/chaotic, Role reversals/boundaries	**Defense mechanisms:** Distortion, Denial/avoidance, Rationalization	**Environment:** Parental violence, Support systems, Economic stress, Sexual attitudes, Intimacy

HISTORY — early childhood experience prior to sexual abuse

Empathic care: Trust, Confident	**Neglectful care:** Emotional, Environmental, Consistency	**Learning styles:** Disability, Opportunity	**Physical abuse:** Acute, Chronic	**Emotional abuse:** Attack, Confusion	**Substance-abusing parents**	**Parental loss:** Illness, Depression, Divorce, Death, Out-of-home placement, Sibling loss	**Rejection:** Betrayal, Abandonment	**Trauma**

Developmental Considerations

Each child's developmental pathway is influenced by the variables in the first three layers of the matrix: what the child brings, what the parents bring, and what happens between them. The group reviewed key concepts relevant to attachment theory (Bowlby, 1969, 1988), the separation-individuation process (Mahler, Pine, & Bergman, 1975), and the developmental crises of trust versus mistrust and autonomy versus shame and doubt (Erikson, 1959) as the basis for exploring the implications of differential developmental pathways. Through the experiences of attachment and separation, the child develops internal representations of self and others characterized by trust or mistrust that guide future interactions between the child's developing personality and his/her expanding environment. As Bowlby (1988) states:

> This means that it is necessary to think of each personality as moving through life along some developmental pathway, with the particular pathway followed always being determined by the interaction of the personality as it has so far developed and the environment in which it then finds itself. (p. 6)

Attachment

A newborn infant is totally helpless and dependent on others to provide adequate care. Developing an attachment relationship with a primary caregiver is a biological imperative or requirement, designed to maintain the physical proximity of the caretaker in order to ensure the survival of the individual (and the species). Human infants are "object seeking" and have an innate need for interpersonal connection in order to survive. These biological, psychological, and social phenomena support an emotional connection to the caregiver that sustains and nurtures the child. Without this emotional connection, infants fail to thrive physically, cognitively, and socially (Spitz, 1945).

The infant's primary attachment relationship becomes internalized over time and becomes the prototype for self-regulation and future relationships. Within the context of these earliest, preverbal relationships, the child develops a set of expectations or beliefs about self and about the world: whether individual needs will be met, whether the world is a safe place, whether others are trustworthy, and whether the child is deserving of attention, affection, and protection. This "internal working model" (Bowlby, 1988) of relationships, of being nurtured and of nurturing, becomes the lens through which all subsequent life experience is perceived.

Several consistent patterns of attachment behavior, reflecting the child's internal working model, have been identified using a research paradigm called the "strange situation," in which researchers observe the reunion behaviors between toddlers and caretakers after a series of separations (Ainsworth & Wittig, 1969). Researchers have described secure, anxious-resistant, anxious-avoidant, and, most recently, disorganized-disoriented patterns of attachment behaviors, based on the way in which the child uses the caregiver as a source of security and comfort (Ainsworth, Blehar, Waters, & Wall, 1978; Main & Solomon, 1990).

Positive, secure attachments develop as a result of empathic parenting. Empathic, sensitive care comes from a parent who is able to recognize accurately and meet adequately the child's needs in a consistent and predictable manner. As the caregiver provides nurturance, stimulation, mirroring, and protection, the child develops a sense of basic trust in the world (Erikson, 1959). Adequately empathic parenting provides the child with the sense that caretakers are available and responsive and will meet the child's needs and that the child is worthwhile, safe, and capable (Delaney, 1991). When the child receives such "good enough" parenting (Winnicott, 1972), a secure attachment, a coherent sense of self, and a positive view of the world can develop.

When caregivers are insensitive, unresponsive, and emotionally or physically inconsistent or unavailable, or when there are significant disruptions in the process of establishing these early relationships, an insecure attachment and a negative view of self and others are likely to develop. Children with an anxious-avoidant attachment behavior pattern show distancing from and avoidance of caretakers upon reunion. Children with an anxious-resistant attachment show an ambivalent, approach-avoidance reaction to caretakers after a separation. Children with insecure attachments have not internalized a secure sense of basic trust in the world or in their own worth or abilities, but they do have an internal working model of relationships. Children raised by extremely abusive, unpredictable parents fail to internalize any working model and exhibit a disorganized-disoriented attachment style. Their behavior reflects their lack of safety and trust in an unpredictable world (George & Solomon, 1989; George, 1993, 1994).

Attachment behavior patterns and the internal working models that develop as a result of early interactions with caretakers are stable over time. The primary attachment relationship becomes internalized over time and becomes the prototype for self-regulation and future relationships with others. The child's initial hypotheses about the world are tested by each new experience, and the child is likely to recreate relationships that confirm this view and avoid or reject experiences that challenge or disconfirm this working model.

Separation-Individuation

According to Mahler, Pine, and Bergman (1975), the child's emerging experience of self as a separate autonomous individual also follows a predictable developmental pattern. Out of the infant's undifferentiated, symbiotic relationship with the mother evolves the toddler's emerging sense of a separate and autonomous self.

The crisis of autonomy (Erikson, 1959) is precipitated by the toddler's developing mobility and an increasing sense of separateness and independence from caregivers. This process follows the previously established attachment pattern in a logical and predictable way. Under positive circumstances, the child uses the caregiver as a secure base from which to explore the ever-expanding world and returns to "refuel" when exploration results in too much separateness, stress, or anxiety (Mahler et al., 1975).

Driven by the child's own developmental needs, separation experiences activate the pattern of attachment behaviors the child has previously learned. This activation may be adaptive or maladaptive, depending on the child's attachment history. Depending on the caregiver's reactions to the push and pull of the child's needs and behaviors at this developmental stage, the child learns to develop a sense of either personal competence and autonomy or shame and self-doubt (Erikson, 1959). Ideally, the child learns to be both close to others and separate and independent from them.

Contextual Considerations

Endowment: What the Child Brings

From the moment of birth, each child is unique. The child brings temperamental, physical, and neurological characteristics that affect the child's contribution to and perception of early relationships and life experiences. Temperament refers to the biological disposition or personality traits that influence the individual's primary style of perceiving, organizing, integrating, and interacting with the world. Thomas and Chess (1977) describe infants as easy, difficult, or slow to warm up, based on variables such as the child's activity level, rhythmicity, threshold of responsiveness, and adaptability. Such traits are thought to remain relatively stable over the life span, exerting a powerful influence on the child's adaptation. Changes or differences over time emerge as a result of the ways the child and the environment moderate or exacerbate the effects of temperamental traits.

The study group hotly debated the role of temperament in attachment. The denial of the uniqueness of each baby at birth contributes to the proliferation of beliefs that all infants' needs are identical and that adequate care can be provided without regard to the individual child's cues. Failure to acknowledge each child's unique endowment and contribution discourages the empathic interchange between mother and infant that enables the development of empathy (Steele, 1989; Ryan, 1995).

While recognizing the importance of each child's individuality, the group emphasized the belief that temperament alone does not determine the quality of a child's attachment to his/her caregivers. A child of any temperament can develop either secure or insecure attachments. In other words, temperament does not determine an infant's confidence in his/her caretakers; sensitive, responsive care, regardless of temperament, does. Mangelsdorf, Gunnar, Kestenbaum, Lang, and Andreas (1990) found no relationship between infants' "proneness-to-distress" (as a temperament trait) at 9 months and their attachment classification at 13 months of age. Temperament, however, was associated with maternal behavior and personality, suggesting that maternal personality has a greater influence on the child's temperament than vice versa. Attachment security was better predicted by an interaction between infant and maternal characteristics than by temperament alone (Mangelsdorf et al., 1990). Bowlby (1988) also criticizes an over-reliance on temperament alone as an explanatory construct:

> [T]he evidence points unmistakably to the conclusion that a host of personal characteristics traditionally described as temperamental and often ascribed to heredity are environmentally induced. True, neonates differ in many ways. Yet the evidence is clear from repeated studies that infants described as difficult during their early days are enabled by sensitive mothers to become happy, easy toddlers. Contrariwise, placid newborns can be turned into anxious, moody, demanding or awkward toddlers by insensitive or rejecting mothering. ... Those who attribute so much to inborn temperament will have to think again. (p. 5)

Physical attributes, such as the child's sex, appearance, or resemblance to family members, affect the child's experience and the response of others. Prematurity and health or medical problems (such as chronic, unsoothable illness or pain) affect the child's needs and may influence the continuity and quality of attachment relationships for better or worse (Brazelton & Cramer, 1990).

The child's intellectual capacity and ability to integrate sensory-motor information and other neurological characteristics similarly affect the child's contribution to and experience of early relationships. It is not known to what extent neurological variables may be shaped by pre- or postnatal influences. It is clear, however, that some heritable predispositions are linked to brain chemistry and that brain chemistry is reactive to life events and experiences. Production of neurotransmitters (which mediate mood, emotion, pain, and pleasure) and the neurological pathways (which influence brain functioning) may vary considerably at birth. Recent research also suggests that for some victims, the intense demand for neurochemical mediators created by the overwhelming emotions

> **Recent research also suggests that for some victims, the intense demand for neurochemical mediators created by the overwhelming emotions associated with trauma can permanently alter chemical brain functions.**

associated with trauma can permanently alter chemical brain functions (Perry, 1993; van der Kolk & Greenberg, 1987).

The complexity of endowment variables suggests that the child's condition at birth will influence the child's functioning and perceptions, which, in turn, will influence relationships with caregivers and affect how the child experiences the world. Every attribute or characteristic the child brings to relationships may either fit or not fit the caregiver's expectations. Similarly, what the child brings to abusive interactions may moderate or exacerbate the harm caused. The empathic mother described by Bowlby (1988) provides care in response to the child's cues, moderating potential difficulties associated with incongruent expectations.

Family of Origin: What the Parents Bring

The infant is born into a preexisting family system that is changed by his/her arrival, and each caregiver brings to the family environment expectations and needs based on his/her own attachment history. The internal working models parents bring to their relationship with the infant are products of their own early childhood experiences. These working models tend to be stable over time, forming the basis for all relationships and becoming the parents' model for caregiving. The strategies parents use to cope with the stresses of child rearing reflect their own experience of being parented (Brazelton & Cramer, 1990; Erickson, Korfmacher, & Egeland, 1992; George, 1994). Each caregiver has his/her own matrix of life experience within which to attempt to make sense of the child's behaviors and provide for the child's needs. The characteristics of the primary caregivers and the environmental qualities and circumstances that surround the child form the context into which the infant is born and within which the infant must interact and adapt in order to survive.

The parents' expectations regarding the child's gender, appearance, temperament, and behavior begin before birth (probably even before conception), based on their own view of themselves and their own experiences as children (Brazelton & Cramer, 1990). Each parent also has expectations about the task of parenting and being nurtured. Parental expectations may be realistic or unreasonably distorted, based on their own experiences of having been parented as children and whether they were nurtured or neglected, appreciated or abused. All these expectations are further affected by whether the child was planned for and wanted, by the circumstances and timing of the child's arrival, and by the parents' internal and external stressors and supports.

Fraiberg, Adelson, and Shapiro (1975) describe the influence of the parents' own childhood experiences as "ghosts in the nursery." They hypothesize that the types of defenses employed by parents in coping with their own childhood experiences are related to the likelihood that they will perpetuate these "ghosts" in raising their own children. The more aware the parents are of painful experiences from childhood, the less likely they are to repeat these same experiences in their own parenting. Parents who do not have access to their own painful feelings due to repression, dissociation, or similar defenses are more at risk for unconsciously repeating their own experiences (Egeland & Susman-Tillman, 1996; Steele, 1989; Haynes-Seman & Kelly, 1988).

The characteristics of the family system, such as boundary cohesion (enmeshed/disengaged) or regulation and adaptability (flexible/rigid/chaotic), reflect the developmental (attachment) history and emotional state of the parents. Within this context, the child may be seen as a unique, separate person or as an extension of the parents' needs and view of themselves. There may be an appreciation of the child's separateness and unique individual needs or the assumption that the child's needs are congruent with or must be subjugated to the parents' or family's needs. Or there may be role reversals in the relationship, with the parents expecting the child to meet their needs.

The parents' coping styles and the defense mechanisms that characterize stress management in the home contribute to family dynamics and become the child's models for coping. Children are exposed to different functional or dysfunctional models of coping with stress or trauma, or, in the absence of any stress or trauma, to no models at all. Children may observe and become a part of a continuum of coping styles ranging from denial, secrecy, or helplessness to competence and functional solutions. The dysfunctional cycle depicted in Chapter 1 represents a learned pattern of stress management that the child may observe throughout childhood. When the modeled responses are based on externalizing defenses and the solutions are compensatory or retaliatory, the child is likely to normalize such patterns and rely on similar solutions when stressed. Subsequently, in dealing with the stress of abuse issues, the risk of control-seeking dysfunctions may be increased.

The quality of the family environment and its support systems (including the extended family) contribute greatly to the quality of the child's development. The child may develop qualities that put him/her at risk due to either the presence of victim characteristics or the absence of protective characteristics.

The child's view of himself/herself and of relationships is colored by exposure to violence and aggression as models of attachment and autonomy. Landry and Peters (1992) present an excellent summary of the development of aggressive conduct problems in young children from an attachment perspective. Bowlby (1985) conceptualizes violence in the family as a consequence of a failure to attach. Similarly, sexual attitudes, the sexual behavior of role models, and sexualized attention significantly affect the child's developing view of attachment, sexuality, and intimacy. Even in the absence of overt sexual abuse, extremely sexualized (Haynes-Seman, 1989) or eroticized (Yates, 1987) parent-child interactions may have precocious influences on the child's developing sexuality. Such children may be at risk from predators who exploit the child's lack of sexual boundaries, or they may develop an oversexualized view of self and others that is reaffirmed in the abuse experience. At the other extreme, the absence or avoidant denial of sexuality in the home environment (Gilgun, 1988; Morris & Bolton, 1986) creates a void in which an experience of sexual victimization becomes the child's only model for understanding sexuality. Such children may also be at risk from any sexual exploitation that appears to offer to fill that void.

Early Childhood Experience Prior to Abuse: What Gets Brought Up

The child has no choice but to move through each developmental stage; the outcomes depend on the interaction of endowment and quality of care. Depending on the variables in each developmental pathway, the child may develop a sense of basic trust in the world and self and a positive sense of independence and autonomy. Or, if these variables do not interact in an expectable, positive manner, the child may develop a sense of mistrust in self, experience, and the world, placing him/her at risk for failure in subsequent developmental tasks.

The child's developmental pathway is shaped by the interaction of endowment, family of origin, and the events that occur within this context. The "goodness of fit" between the child's temperament and parental and familial characteristics is an important variable in the developmental outcome of these interactions (Chess & Thomas, 1984). Some temperamental traits are referred to as "difficult" due to conflicts or tension created by the traits that affect the child's ability to "fit" the expectations of parents and others (Ryan, 1995). Special needs of the infant related to endowment characteristics may create stress for the caregiver. Empathic parenting depends on the parents' ability to understand their child's unique personality and temperament and meet his/her needs accordingly. Empathic parents work at understanding their child's style — even when it is different from their own — and at establishing a nurturing "fit" that will enable a secure attachment relationship. When parents have not received empathic, nurturing parenting themselves, this process may be seriously compromised unless other mediating experiences have intervened.

A child's attachment history may be relatively positive and smooth, guided by empathic parenting and free from external trauma, or it may be marked by disruptions related to parental loss, rejection, neglect, abuse, or exposure to violence. Whatever is happening around the child also affects the child. For example, maternal depression has been correlated with childhood problems and developmental psychopathology (Cummings & Cicchetti, 1990). Disruptions in early relationships may be coincidental in the parent-child relationship (e.g., divorce, parental hospitalization or incarceration, job circumstances) yet may profoundly jeopardize the child's developing sense of basic trust, secure attachments, and a healthy, positive view of self and others. According to Bowlby (1988, p. 3), "a failure in response of his familiar caregiver, whether due to physical absence or a failure to respond appropriately, should always cause stress and sometimes be traumatic."

Even in the absence of overt trauma, the extent to which the child must adapt to the parent — rather than experience the validation of a nurturing, empathic environment — may jeopardize the development of empathy and trust for self and others. "The greater the demands for the child to accommodate to the mother rather than vice versa, the greater the costs to the child in terms of distortions of temperamental characteristics and ... developmental needs" (Lieberman & Paul, 1990, p. 395).

From the beginning, this study group was profoundly appreciative of Roland Summit's seminal paper on the child sexual abuse accommodation syndrome (1983). His recognition that the actual abuse the child experienced was only one discrete variable in describing the subsequent effects opened the door to exploration of the child's struggle to integrate the abuse experience into his or her contextual experience and to defend against negative effects.

Attachment and Abuse

Secure attachments predict more positive outcomes across many developmental domains and may be a protective factor in coping with abuse, contributing to a positive adaptation or outcome because the child has had the opportunity to internalize empathic experiences that can be called on to provide soothing and strength in times of stress or trauma. Also, the environment that supported the development of the child's attachment is likely to be continuous over time, to offer the same quality of care. At the same time, the securely attached child may be more likely to experience abuse as dystonic or incongruent with the internal working model, and the experience of abuse may be more traumatic because of this dissonance. But the securely attached child may be better prepared to express and manage the emotional and cognitive effects. Any discontinuity in parental care or response, a failure to protect or the inability to respond empathically, would contribute to the dissonance of the abuse and affect outcomes.

Attachment is a biological and psychological imperative, and it occurs regardless of the quality of parental care. The child is dependent on parental care for survival and must adapt to parental demands and needs in order to survive, even when the attachment jeopardizes healthful development. The most obvious and severe failures in parenting are apparent in psychological, physical, or sexual abuse. These developmental disruptions or failures become internalized and incorporated into the child's sense of self and expectations of the world.

Significant disruptions in the child's primary attachments appear to increase the risk of vulnerability to stressful life events, including sexual abuse. For example, children without a secure base of attachment and safety may be even more vulnerable to the issues of safety and protection involved in sexual abuse. Disruptions in the attachment process interfere with the child's developing self-regulation and relatedness to others, affecting both the child's experience of abuse and his/her subsequent ability to cope by self-soothing and by seeking safety and comfort from others. Chronic abuse may further reinforce the child's

> **Attachment is a biological and psychological imperative, and it occurs regardless of the quality of parental care.**

already negative view of self and others and may be incorporated into a view of abuse as syntonic with life experience, as expressed by such statements as "I deserve it" or "That's life."

An insecure attachment may be a risk factor in the outcome of childhood sexual abuse for two reasons: First, the child's insecurity becomes internalized in a negative working model through which he/she attempts to understand, adapt to, and cope with life experiences. Second, the problems contributing to an insecure attachment — some disruption in either the goodness of fit between the parent and child or the consistency of "good enough" parenting — are likely to continue after the experience of abuse. Such disruptions are in themselves risk factors in addition to the abuse. Moreover, an avoidantly or resistantly attached child is likely to respond to caregivers with these behavior patterns, and caregivers are likely to respond in the manner that contributed initially to the child's insecure attachment. For the severely attachment-disordered child, the experience of abuse may be congruent with his/her internal working model and be experienced as less traumatic, but the child's options and models for coping are likely to be less functional, perhaps characterized by externalizing and/or compensatory solutions.

In the context of a healthy attachment relationship, a hurt or injured child runs to the parent for comfort. When a child is instead hurt or exploited by that parent, there may be no safe haven, resulting in the disorganized-disoriented attachment patterns identified by researchers (Main & Solomon, 1990). For these children, there is no safe or reliable response to separations or reunions with caregivers. Trauma may be congruent with the child's internal working model, but only because it is inescapable. If the only one to whom the children can turn for help in defining the abuse experience or in seeking comfort and nurturance is the perpetrator of the abuse, the child's understanding will certainly include the distortions and rationalizations of the perpetrator. The traumatic effects of child abuse and neglect on attachment and developmental tasks are dramatically described by Judith Herman (1992):

> In this climate of profoundly disrupted relationships the child faces a formidable developmental task. She must find a way to form primary attachments to caretakers who are either dangerous or, from her perspective, negligent. She must find a way to develop a sense of basic trust and safety with caretakers who are untrustworthy and unsafe. She must develop a sense of self in relation to others who are helpless, uncaring or cruel. She must develop a capacity for bodily self-regulation in an environment in which her body is at the disposal of others' needs, as well as a capacity for self-soothing in an environment without solace. She must develop the capacity for initiative in an environment which demands that she bring her will into complete conformity with that of her abuser. And ultimately, she must develop a capacity for intimacy out of an environment where all intimate relationships are corrupt, and identity out of an environment which defines her as a whore and a slave. (p. 101)

Obviously, if abuse is occurring within the family context, within the child's primary attachment relationship, the quality of the attachment is severely compromised. This may be the most devastating impact of such abuse. Abuse within the context of family relationships may be perceived as a "normal" part of family life, or even as an expression of love and affection. If trusted family members define it as normal, the child may have to adopt this view in order to preserve the attachment relationship. Many children idealize abusive parents and distort their perceptions to attribute blame to themselves or others rather than to the responsible parent in order to preserve a desperately needed attachment relationship of dubious quality. As Herman (1992) writes:

In the course of normal development, a child achieves a secure sense of autonomy by forming inner representations that can be evoked mentally in times of distress. ... In a climate of chronic childhood abuse, these inner representations cannot form in the first place; they are repeatedly, violently shattered by traumatic experience. Unable to develop an inner sense of safety, the abused child remains more dependent on external sources of comfort and solace. Unable to develop a secure sense of independence, the abused child continues to seek desperately and indiscriminately for someone to depend upon. The result is a paradox, observed repeatedly in abused children, that while they quickly become attached to strangers, they also cling tenaciously to the very parents who mistreat them. (p. 107)

There may, however, be mitigating factors in the child's life experience after the abuse — including the child's coping or survival skills — that help ameliorate both the impact of the sexual abuse and the previous ego injuries related to disruptions in the attachment or separation processes. Mrazek and Mrazek (1987) discuss both "generic" and "abuse-specific" protective factors related to the general context of the child's life and the specific events following disclosure of sexual abuse. Resilient children, who do well in spite of abuse, are able to interpret parental failures as the parent's problem and not their own and do better than those who internalize blame for the inadequate care they receive (Mrazek & Mrazek, 1987). Current formulations also emphasize the continuity of external protective factors, such as mentoring relationships, in overcoming the impact of abuse (Katz, 1997).

Over the years, the study group has continued to believe that a developmental approach to child sexual abuse is essential in understanding the impact of each victim's experience and his/her resources for adaptation. The context within which the abuse occurs, the child's history before and after the abuse, and the developmental stage at which the abuse occurs may combine to influence the unique developmental pathway for each child. We hypothesize that the developmental stage or stages at which the child is abused may determine which areas of functioning are most affected by the disruption of stage-related developmental tasks. The accommodation and assimilation of the individual's unique perceptions within the context of prior life experience may predict whether the child experiences long-term sequelae.

Developmental research on the effects of childhood sexual abuse is in its infancy (Downs, 1993). Much of the research to date has focused on discrete variables but has found that the effects of abuse vary among individuals at the time of the abuse (Browne & Finkelhor, 1986) as well as within individuals over time (Downs, 1993). Identification of increasingly negative effects for some victims over time suggests that some developmental needs may be "bypassed or short circuited as victims pass through later stages of development" in a process Downs (1993, p. 333) refers to as "progressive accumulation."

Finkelhor and Dziuba-Leatherman's (1994) proposal for the study of developmental victimology is congruent with our group's beliefs. They hypothesize that the "nature, quantity, and impact of victimization ... vary across childhood with the different capabilities, activities and environments that are characteristic of different stages of development" (p.178). They suggest that the effects of victimization can be differentiated by the degree to which they are related to the unique dependency status of children. As discussed earlier, dependency is based primarily on the biological and psychological need for attachment relationships. Finkelhor and Dziuba-Leatherman conclude with a call for a more developmental perspective in research on child victimization that will help to "differentiate how children, with all their individual differences, react and cope at different stages with the challenges posed by victimization. It is only through this more differentiated approach that we can understand how victimization leaves its mark on children's lives" (p. 182).

Understanding each child's attachment history and subsequent developmental pathways provides a theoretical model for a developmental understanding of the unique impact and differential outcomes of sexual abuse. By exploring the possible impact of childhood sexual abuse on the developmental tasks of basic trust, autonomy, and identity in a developmental context, the implications for subsequent developmental tasks and the need for differential treatment strategies become clear.

4

The Experience and Effect of Sexual Abuse and Trauma

Gizane Indart

There is no single syndrome that reflects the impact of sexual abuse

—*Kendall-Tackett, Williams, & Finkelhor, 1993, p. 170*

I t is apparent that victims of sexual abuse display many different outcomes. Sexual abuse does not result in a consistent cluster of symptoms (Kendall-Tackett, Williams, & Finkelhor, 1993). The same experience, in different children, can be manifested in disparate immediate and long-term sequelae. With one child, for instance, depression and diminished self-esteem can be predominant. With another child, sexualized behaviors are the prevailing symptoms. This proposition leads to another: that children cannot be adequately understood unless they are appreciated as developing entities who must be evaluated and treated in the context of their whole life experiences.

The ways that victims of sexual abuse give meaning to their experience are colored by the individual's previous developmental history, including the quality of the child's attachment patterns discussed in Chapter 3. Within this context, the development of coping mechanisms and behavioral manifestations following the experience of sexual victimization reflects the perceptual differences of individual phenomenology and history.

Sexual abuse is not a disorder, it is a life event: a negative experience that many persons suffer, leading to a vast array of outcomes.

Terr (1991) uses the following analogy to illustrate childhood trauma:

> Like rheumatic fever, childhood trauma creates changes that may even-
> tually lead to a number of different diagnoses. But also like rheumatic
> fever, childhood trauma must always be kept in mind as a possible
> underlying mechanism when these various conditions appear. (p. 19)

Potential sequelae, negative effects, and outcomes are some of the terms used in this chapter to describe and discuss the impact of the experience of sexual victimization and the changes that it may impose on victims. Specifically explored are the effects and clinical manifestations that the experience of sexual abuse may bring to the person, as depicted in Figure 4.1.

The chapter begins with a theoretical discussion defining trauma. Next, we explore the negative sequelae of sexual abuse, and finally describe the unique ways that victims of sexual abuse attempt to cope with this experience. Case vignettes are used to exemplify the ideas conveyed.

Trauma

In a sense, Freud turned away from the millions of victims of sexual abuse of this world when he shifted his position. Freud also failed to understand that trauma can be originated by either internal or external conflict, or by a combination of both.

Different theories of trauma have dominated the literature of sexual abuse since the last century, from Freud in the 1890s through Terr (1990a, 1990b, 1994) in the present and her conceptualization of trauma types I and II. In his writings before 1896 (specifically, *Studies on Hysteria* with Joseph Breuer, 1895/1955), Sigmund Freud hypothesized that we repress some memories because they cause us painful conflict. Sexual abuse in childhood is the conflicted event that accounts for repression, Freud stated. But after 1896 (with the publication of *The Aetiology of Hysteria*), Freud turned away from real events in the

Figure 4.1 Issues, Characteristics, and Behaviors Over-represented in Short-Term Outcomes

OUTCOMES		
Issues: anxiety; humiliation; lack of control; helplessness, vulnerability, powerlessness; embarrassment, shame, guilt; put down, betrayed, devalued; post-traumatic stress; loss; confusion: sexual, cognitive, role boundary, relationship	**Characteristics:** poor self-image, lack of trust, distorted thinking, negative expectations; rejection, failure, personalizing sexual offense, depersonalizing others, preoccupation, depression, fear of intimacy, sadness, deviant sexual arousal, indiscriminate external locus of control	**Manifestations:** setting self up, power/control behaviors, phobias, withdrawal, isolating, P.T.S.D., unrealistic expectations, unrealistic behaviors, thinking errors, putting self down, somatic complaints, attention deficit, learning disability, promiscuity, aggression, self-destructive behavior, sexual acting out, sexual abuse perpetration/revictimization

lives of patients, considering instead that children's fantasies of being seduced and the internal conflicts they cause are the reason that people repress. In a sense, Freud turned away from the millions of victims of sexual abuse of this world when he shifted his position. Freud also failed to understand that trauma can be originated by either internal or external conflict, or by a combination of both.

In the mid-1950s, Freud's daughter Anna brought together different lines of thought regarding childhood trauma. In 1981 she wrote:

> Far from existing only as a phantasy, incest is thus also a fact, more widespread among the population in certain periods than in others. Where the chances of harming a child's normal developmental growth are concerned, it ranks higher than abandonment, neglect, physical maltreatment, or any other form of abuse. It would be a fatal mistake to underrate either the importance or the frequency of its actual occurrence. (p. 34)

In this way, Anna Freud filled in the space left by her father when he proposed the seduction theory in lieu of real-life experiences.

Anna Freud presents another dimension in the comprehension of traumatic events. She hypothesized trauma as a state in which the ego is "overwhelmed" and "flooded" by more stimuli than it can manage. Steele (1991) explains Anna Freud's perspective while discussing her writing:

> Even if the neonate is considered protected against excessive stimulation by a high threshold of excitation, the older infant may be thought of as potentially traumatized all the time since his rudimentary ego has no ability to cope with overstimulation from either external or internal sources. What comes to his rescue normally are the ministrations of his mother who, by providing care, protection, and comfort, assumes the role of a protective shield, holds off external excitations, and alleviates internal stimuli. It is only in the second year of life that this function of the protective shield (or auxiliary ego) gradually passes over from the mother to the child himself and is taken over by his own ego. (p. 37)

During our monthly meetings, it was Dr. Steele who frequently reminded group members that "trauma occurs if either the stimulus is too great or the shield is too weak, or there is a combination of both."

In the mid-1950s, a new interest in childhood trauma began to emerge when David Levy, a psychiatrist from New York, compared childhood trauma with the battlefield trauma suffered by soldiers in the Second World War.

Between 1977 and 1981, Terr studied the children who were kidnapped from their school bus in Chowchilla in 1976. Terr reported that every one of the kidnapped children retained detailed, precise memories of what had happened, even four years later. The Chowchilla children consistently remembered everything. Nobody forgot or repressed this traumatic memory. This study, along with two others — a retrospective study of 20 preschoolers suffering from a wide range of traumas that were documented by third parties (1988), and a study of normal latency-aged children's responses to the *Challenger* space shuttle explosion (1990a) — laid out Terr's theoretical foundation to conceptualize childhood trauma. In the paper "Childhood Traumas: An Outline and Overview" (1991), Terr provides a definition of "trauma" that the group found particularly valuable: "The mental result of one sudden external blow, or series of blows, rendering the young person temporarily helpless and breaking past ordinary coping and defense operations" (p. 11). Terr's work reflects not only the original Freudian conceptualization of trauma, but also the conditions marked by prolonged anticipation (S. Freud, 1920). Her appreciation of the child's expectation of further abuse parallels Hindman's (1989) descriptions of survivors' accounts of anticipatory dread.

Terr's research explores childhood traumas that originate from the acts of others. Trauma cannot be generated solely within the child's own mind. Once the situation occurs, cognitive and emotional changes take place internally as the child attempts to understand and give meaning to the experience. Terr proposes that childhood traumas can be divided into two main categories. According to Terr's classification, type I traumas are conditions that follow an unexpected, unanticipated external blow:

> Those children who suffer the results of single blows appear to exhibit certain symptoms and signs that differentiate their conditions from those resulting from the more complicated events. The findings special to single, shocking, intense terrors are 1) full, detailed, etched-in memories, 2) "omens" (retrospective reworkings, cognitive reappraisals, reasons, and turning points), and 3) misperceptions and mistimings. Type I traumas do not appear to breed the massive denials, psychic numbings, self-anesthesias, or personality problems that characterize the type II disorders of childhood. (Terr, 1991, p. 14)

The Chowchilla children provide a good example of type I trauma, showing no impairment in their ability to retrieve detailed and full memories of the incident.

In contrast, type II traumas are the conditions that follow long-standing or repeated exposure to traumatic events. In Terr's words:

> The first such event, of course, creates surprise. But the subsequent unfolding of horrors creates a sense of anticipation. Massive attempts to protect the psyche and to preserve the self are put into gear. The defenses and coping operations used in the type II disorders of childhood — massive denial, repression, dissociation, self-anesthesia, self-hypnosis, identification with the aggressor, and aggression turned against the self — often lead to profound character changes in the youngster. (p. 15)

The repeatedly abused and traumatized child often seen in long-term residential care exhibits the effects of this type of trauma. These children have constructed and internalized a negative working model of themselves and the world prior to the sexual abuse experience, considering themselves as unworthy and unlovable and others as unresponsive and unreliable. The injuries inflicted to their self-development may have been profound and chronic from early in life or may have been acute events that arrested or distorted normative developmental tasks. For these children, the experience of sexual abuse may further reinforce and compound their negative view of self and others. The abuse in these cases may be congruent, consistent, and syntonic with their prior life experiences.

EXAMPLE 1:
By the time Marjorie was referred to long-term residential treatment, she had developed a wide variety of maladaptive behaviors and defensive strategies. Marjorie suffered long-standing abuse, neglect, and malnourishment while living with her parents, who were consistently described by different mental health professionals as highly abusive, unempathic sufferers of severe mental psychopathology. Early in life, Marjorie became her own caretaker, developing several "pseudo-selves" to protect herself from further emotional injuries. Marjorie presented as superficially charming and engaging, always ready to conform and please others. She relied heavily on her well-developed façade, needing external cues to understand other people's behaviors, thoughts, and feelings, probably as an overcompensation for her diminished sense of self and fragile identity. For Marjorie, internal psychological injuries and an accumulation of damage occurred from the time she was born. When Marjorie's sexual victimization began, she had already internalized a negative view of herself as unworthy and unlovable and of adults as uncaring and unresponsive to her needs. Marjorie's sexual victimization confirmed and reinforced her negative working model.

By its very nature, trauma is the occurrence of the unthinkable. Cognitively, a traumatic blow occurs outside the range of what the human mind expects. Therefore, the child cannot assimilate the experience because it is incongruent with past experience; the child cannot developmentally accommodate the meaning of the experience without revising his/her schema of the world.

A traumatic event creates dissonance in a person's life. A Japanese proverb wonderfully captures this idea: Trauma stops time. Every year since the detonation of nuclear bombs wreaked havoc on the cities of Hiroshima and Nagasaki, thousands of Japanese have congregated on the anniversary of the bombing to mourn their dead and express their pain, exemplifying the existence of a definite "before" and "after" the traumatic experience that affected and changed their nation as a whole.

Young (1992) states that any traumatic event violates the most basic assumptions about the self and the world: that I am invulnerable (both a physical and a psychological assumption of competence); that I am good and worthy (internal mental representation of self); that I deserve good things to happen to me (worthiness); and that the world and others are trustworthy (basic trust or confidence). Therefore, the violation of sexual abuse crosses the boundary between inside the person and outside the person (against the person's will) and entails cognitive, physical, psychological, interpersonal, and social intrusion.

> **Not every child initially perceives the experience of sexual abuse as traumatic because the victim may be interpreting the experience as a normal, congruent way to get close to others, as a style of relatedness, and so forth.**

The saying that trauma stops time captures the essence of discontinuity, incongruence, and dissonance. These constructs support the position that not all sexual abuse experiences are traumatic for the person who experiences them. In other words, not every child initially perceives the experience of sexual abuse as traumatic because the victim may be interpreting the experience as a normal, congruent way to get close to others, as a style of relatedness, and so forth. It is possible that through the experience of sexual abuse, this child found and received the nurturance, intimacy, attention, and closeness not otherwise available.

EXAMPLE 2:

At age 14, Ted was referred for treatment following a brief history of sibling incest with his 8-year-old sister. Ted's mother was 14 when he was born, and throughout his life, her primary interest has been seducing new lovers as a means of avoiding being alone. Five younger children were the product of the mother's sexualized lifestyle, but the maintenance of multiple sexual relationships left her little time or energy for parenting them. Consequently, Ted was cast in the role of caregiver for five vulnerable children. The sexualization of the sibling relationship was a natural extension of Ted's internalized representation of his role model's world. His mother's relationships were so sexualized that he immediately sexualized his relationships with peers as well, engaging same-sex peers in sexualized horseplay, jokes, and innuendo, and approaching opposite-sex peers as sexual objects to be seduced. His motives were not abusive or retaliatory, and the function of his behavior was not so much compensatory as simply normalized. In Ted's mind, love and sadism, nurturance and abuse, are understandably paired, as this paradox is congruent and syntonic with his previous life experiences. Such patterns were extremely resistant to change, however, due to the pervasive, phenomenological quality of his sexualized self-image.

It is clear that early in life Ted was engaged in role-reversed interactions with his mother, wherein his role in the family was to meet the physical and emotional needs of his mother and siblings. When role-reversed interactions include the sexualization of the parent-child relationship, the eroticized child may internalize the idea that this is the way relationships are developed and established and may have the tendency to repeat the same pattern of interaction in subsequent relationships. Often the eroticized child has internalized a high value for sexual cues, having learned vicariously that sexual relationships are more highly valued than any others by the parental figure.

Although Ted's initial coping skills and style of relatedness served the purpose of accommodating to parental dysfunction, over time it became dysfunctional due to overgeneralization, which led to deviant sexual behaviors. Deviant behaviors are in themselves a harmful effect. Although Ted may not have initially perceived his eroticized relationship with his mother and his siblings as traumatic, the normalization of aberrant, potentially harmful behaviors establishes the harmful or traumatic nature of his own developmental experience as well as the ultimate confusion for his victims.

The sexual abuse experience is not necessarily traumatic in and of itself. It is the quality of the relationship and interaction that defines the sexual experience as abuse (Ryan et al., 1988). Not every child perceives sexual abuse as traumatic, as is apparent in the case examples of Ted and Charles (below). When the experience of abuse brings incongruence, discontinuity, and disruption to the developmental path, it is likely to be perceived as a traumatic experience. The abuse that is most dissonant in an individual's life is the abuse that is most likely to be experienced as traumatic by the person who suffers from it.

EXAMPLE 3:
Charles was adopted as an infant by parents who had an idealized mental representation of themselves as parents, but whose relationship lacked any sense of intimacy. Although Charles received all the "required" physical care to grow and develop, emotionally and relationally he grew up in a sterile environment void of any models of attachment, intimacy, or sexuality. His parents rarely touched each

other and set very distant physical boundaries with Charles as well, in keeping with the father's mental representation of males as defended and self-contained. Genital or sexual curiosity was extinguished through avoidance and religious disapproval, and Charles grew up like a small ship alone in the sea, without any sense of intimacy or empathy, unable to touch or nurture himself or others.

With the onset of puberty, sexual urges and the push for autonomy found him lacking any internal representation of intimate relationships, and he began enticing younger boys at the mall into hidden corners, where he would (quite clumsily) attempt to hug them and rub his genitals against them. He lacked the empathy to perceive the distress he caused and experienced a temporary sense of intimacy that was both exciting and shameful for him. His behavior was reinforcing enough to become rapidly habituated, and the push to repeat the behavior was urgent, even after he was arrested. In the parents' view, responsibility for the development of Charles's paraphilia was attributed to the birth parents as an inborn trait.

Charles's situation demonstrates the dilemma of the child in an "asexual" environment. The onset of sexual urges at puberty was experienced as traumatic by Charles because it was dystonic and incongruent to his previous developmental history. The "sexual neglect" Charles was exposed to in his home environment (with his adoptive parents) profoundly damaged his sensual and relational development. Charles's paraphilia illustrates the trauma of early and ongoing neglect rather than suggesting that the cause was normal developmental challenges.

The Impact of Sexual Abuse

Three models of trauma, the post-traumatic stress disorder (PTSD) model (McLeer, Deblinger, Atkins, Foa, & Ralphe, 1988), the traumagenic factors model (Finkelhor & Browne, 1985), and the information processing of trauma (IPT) model (Hatman & Burgess, 1993), have been useful in understanding the impact of sexual abuse on children. The PTSD model emphasizes the traumatic nature of sexual abuse in a fairly constant set of cognitive and behavioral effects, including intrusive thoughts, numbing, hyperarousal, and avoidance of the triggering events. The PTSD model is the one that directly correlates to treatment practice. Treatment techniques derived from the PTSD model include anxiety reduction strategies as well as cognitive reprogramming.

The PTSD model would be much more useful if the majority of sexually abused children presented with PTSD as a diagnosis. According to Friedrich's (1995) review of the literature on the impact of sexual abuse in children, the percentage of sexually abused children ($N = 151$ children from four studies) with symptoms of PTSD ranged from 18 to 68 percent. These data indicate that not all clinically identified child victims meet the diagnostic criteria for PTSD (Kendall-Tackett et al., 1993; McLeer et al., 1988). This conclusion leads to another: the recognition that many child victims who experience serious and lasting effects suffer from problems that are not readily encompassed within the PTSD model.

The traumagenic factors model (Finkelhor & Browne, 1985) awakened enormous interest among clinicians, who are often captivated by the notion of trauma and its potentially disabling effects. Finkelhor & Browne (1985) suggested that sexual abuse is pernicious or harmful because of four traumatic factors: betrayal, stigmatization, powerlessness, and traumatic sexualization. Each of these traumagenic factors has a potential impact on both overt behavior and internal psychological processes, including cognitions. This theory is very helpful in identifying the wide range of possible treatment needs and suggests that the field of child sexual abuse needs to move beyond an exclusive focus on trauma, which creates blinders (Cummings & Cicchetti, 1990). As Friedrich (1995) affirms:

> Victims must be defined by more than their victim history. Not to do so is to belittle them. Not to do so also removes us from the numerous useful theories that can drive our research and therapy so that we can become better informed and more effective practitioners. (p. 3).

The IPT model is a neuropsychosocial model that describes how information is experienced, filtered, and related to the process of memory, retrieval, and recall when trauma occurrs. The IPT model emphasizes the hyperarousal inherent in the trauma (Hartman & Burgess, 1993). The theory is that the limbic system of the brain is overwhelmed by the traumatic event. Consequently, key processes in the construction of memory for the event and in subsequent learning are disrupted. This disruption of normal memory processes gives rise, for example, to dissociation and repression of traumatic events. Because defense mechanisms are invisible, they are more likely to be overlooked or disregarded. At times, trauma results in clearly visible scars, while at other times, equally traumatic injury remains unseen. Therefore, it is important to refrain from assuming that a lack of overt symptoms suggests that no trauma was inflicted.

> To assume that an absence of symptoms is indicative of no traumatic scars is as erroneous as assuming that the experience of sexual victimization is always traumatic. The absence of symptoms, in many cases, constitutes the symptom.

Study group members have been struggling with the question of what constitutes trauma. In our monthly meetings at the Kempe Center, different opinions have been voiced. To assume that an absence of symptoms is indicative of no traumatic scars is as erroneous as assuming that the experience of sexual victimization is always traumatic. The absence of symptoms, in many cases, constitutes the symptom. As Terr (1991, p. 4) so clearly postulates, "Even those children who do manage to evade posttraumatic stress syndromes may still hold their terrible experiences as unassimilable 'foreign Objects' in otherwise well-integrated lives." Terr dedicates an entire book, *Unchained Memories* (1994), to the study of traumatic memories that were lost and sometimes found. In the prologue, Terr writes:

> A deluge of letters hit my desk in the summer of 1990, in response to my first book, *Too Scared to Cry*, which dealt with the effect of trauma on children. These letters … showed me what a wide array of defenses exists to keep adults from recalling the horrors they experienced as children. And they showed me what a wide variety of ways there are for these memories to return. The letter writers also showed me that a whole life can be shaped by an old trauma, remembered or not. A woman wrote that she spent eight years as a cloistered nun — her means of unconsciously repressing memories of sexual abuse she had suffered as a child. A man wrote of being misdiagnosed as schizophrenic; his lost memories had made his behavior entirely incomprehensible to his therapists, who knew nothing of the childhood incidents that led to it. Another man wrote of running a marathon, reviewing his life in the process, and finding a number of old memories that

explained not only certain lifelong fears but also his choice of profession. Some of these letters described how old childhood memories had reappeared — through dream watching, poetry writing, painting, keeping journals. Some of the writers had become amateur detectives, asking questions of old friends or family members, checking out back issues of newspapers and area maps. And a few had gone back to their original family homes, in order to see again the places where their memories took root. (p. xii)

The three theories are not completely separate but overlap somewhat. All three models include a belief in the traumatic nature of sexual abuse and in the existence of a wide range of sequelae ranging from minimal to severe.

These three theories have proved helpful, particularly when the issue of sexual abuse initially came to the fore. They also have limitations, however, including the fact that these theories emphasize one or two aspects of the sexual abuse experience but disregard the person as a whole. A second problem is their sole emphasis on the individual victim without addressing the developmental, social, and family context in which children are embedded. According to Friedrich (1995, p. 6):

> The sexually abused child cannot be considered outside a family context. Although there is no denying the traumatic potential of sexual abuse, research increasingly points to family variables, including support for the child, as strongly associated with the effect of abuse. ... Other clinical literature describes the PTSD-like reactions that some parents have regarding their child's sexual abuse. ... These facts do not negate the unique impact of sexual abuse. However, I believe that individually based theories on impact are not sufficient either to understand the impact or to guide the type of broad-based treatment that is needed.

In his book *Psychotherapy with Sexually Abused Boys* (1995), Friedrich proposes an integrated model that broadens the understanding of the impact of sexual abuse. Friedrich's integrated and contextual model borrows from three well-developed theoretical perspectives: attachment theory (Alexander, 1993), regulation of behaviors and emotions (Dodge & Garber, 1992), and self-representation (Crittendon, 1992; Harter, 1983). The effect and impact of sexual abuse are reflected in each of these three broad domains. Further, Friedrich (1995) writes:

The integrated model subsumes the traumagenic factors, information processing, and the PTSD models and provides an additional developmental and family context. For example, the traumagenic factor of betrayal (Finkelhor & Browne, 1985) has both psychological and behavioral effects. These include distrust of others and an impaired ability to form close relationships. Both of these effects are clearly relevant to attachment theory. Stigmatization and powerlessness have behavioral and psychological sequelae that include reduced self-efficacy and a distorted view of self. Each of these is directly related to how the child or adolescent perceives himself. Finally, the traumatic nature of sexual abuse affects the child's ability to regulate his emotions, thoughts, and behaviors, leading to some of the specific symptoms outlined in the PTSD and information-processing models and is suggestive of dysregulation. In addition, sexual abuse is the abuse of the relationship, and the degree to which it influences prior attachments or is reflective of problematic prior attachments makes its effects pertinent to attachment theory as well. (p. 7)

While the search for a causal effect evolved into a more integrated and holistic approach to understanding the uniqueness of the sexual abuse experience, a parallel process occurred within the group. Frequently, we found ourselves searching for the "magic recipe" that could be applied to all clients. As Ryan and her associates write in Chapter 2, this temptation is greatly influenced by two important factors: the clinician's internal need to avoid the pain and the time-consuming process of eliciting the life experience and phenomenology of each client, and the external pressure on the clinician to provide a "quick fix" through short-term therapies. Gradually, a process of integration and articulation began to emerge. In the preface, Ryan suggests that the group's integrative process illustrates how the group has gone full circle: we began by viewing sexual abuse as a uniquely different and devastating phenomenon of human experience and developing theories and therapies specific to the problem; eventually we reached an understanding that what is most unique is the individual client; and now we're returning to theories and therapies regarding human development and therapeutic relationships.

Group members have come to the realization that there is no one-to-one correlation between the traumatic event and the outcome. What may appear from an adult perspective to be a relatively benign experience can be traumatizing to a particular child. Conversely, a child exposed to a highly stressful event may not comprehend the danger and may feel relatively safe.

The group has hypothesized that an assessment of traumatization should take into consideration both the child's experience and the meanings that the child attributes to that experience. The meaning is colored by the child's previous life experiences (psychosocial history, temperament, level of development, style of relatedness), by the context in which the event occurred, and by the response from significant attachment figures. The marker and the outcome of a traumatic situation are not determined by the event but by the meaning that the child gives to that particular event.

Behavioral Manifestations and Sequelae of Sexual Abuse

The study group has hypothesized that the different coping strategies children develop to manage and interpret the experience of abuse are intrinsically related to their internal representational models of themselves and the world. The representational model is the way an individual perceives, interprets, and responds to future life experiences (Bowlby, 1980). Such a construct "may both explain the development of the various coping strategies that children use, and also provide a basis for understanding the coherence of behavioral manifestations" (Crittendon, 1992, p. 330).

The term "coping" denotes the intrapsychic processes and their concurrent behaviors that represent each individual's unique way of dealing with stressful experiences. Coping is described as a dynamic process, a set of constantly changing cognitive and behavioral efforts to manage specific external and/or internal demands that are perceived as exceeding or overwhelming the resources of the individual. In the study group, Dr. Steele frequently reminded us that it is not the bad experiences of life that make us vulnerable, but rather a lack of resources to cope effectively with the stress created by the experiences.

Traumatic sexual victimization "forces" victims to either reject or recreate reality so as to make sense of such experience. Rejection may be accomplished by dissociating from either the past reality or the present experience. Reorganization or rearrangement of previous beliefs about reality allows the victim to find and give meaning to the experience of abuse.

The group's hypothesis is that the ways in which victims cope with the experience of abuse are exquisitely unique and are embodied in the context of the whole life experience: their views of themselves and of the world. There are as many different ways of dealing with an abusive experience as there are individuals who are abused. The responsibility of the professional is to help clients discover the meaning and significance they have attached to the experience and to invite clients to explore the utility of that view.

In attempts to understand and give meaning to abusive experiences, victims develop coping mechanisms and protective strategies that serve many purposes, paramount being the need to survive. Defense mechanisms and their accompanying behavioral manifestations are normal, adaptive human responses to stress, designed to ensure psychological survival. Victims use defenses in an attempt to alleviate the stress of feeling vulnerable and to regain a sense of control following experiences perceived as overwhelming and uncontrollable. These defenses, along with their behavioral manifestations, serve as a protective barrier against feeling vulnerable and out of control. The patterns represented in the cycle in Chapter 1 are common reactions to stress that become dysfunctional only when the behavior is abusive or the stressor is not resolved. The behaviors may appear extreme because the stressor (feelings associated with the abuse) remains a secret, but the pattern represents the expression of the mind's search for a solution to the unsolvable (an attempt to master or erase the impact of traumatic experience). See Figure 4.2.

> **These behavior problems can now be understood from this perspective: they are expectable and logical survival responses.**

The potential symptoms share common emotional, psychosomatic, and behavioral features that are extensively described in the literature as manifest in the short term by children who were sexually abused. These behavioral problems can now be understood from this perspective: they are expectable and logical survival responses.

EXAMPLE 4:
Lauren, a 6-year-old, was adopted after three prior foster home placements. Superficially compliant, Lauren was passive and peaceable but

Figure 4.2   Pattern Associated with Dysfunctional Coping

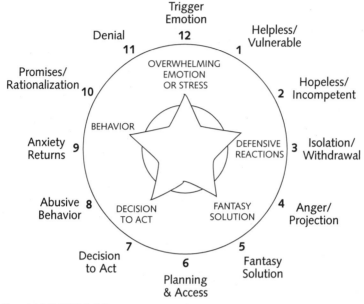

Copyright © 1998 Gail Ryan

also quietly vengeful, with many secret ways of meeting her psychic and emotional needs. Her social history revealed exposure to frightening episodes of physical and sexual abuse and ongoing domestic violence. As a toddler, Lauren had been thrown against the wall twice by her father, once sustaining a skull fracture. She was repeatedly sexually abused by her father from age 1 until she was removed from her parents' home at age 3½. Lauren had also witnessed her father put a gun to her mother's head as a result of a domestic dispute.

Lauren learned to avoid her father and to "read" his moods. Since speaking up, fighting back, or complaining was so dangerous, she learned to keep silent. Lauren never expressed discontent, desire, or difference of opinion around her father. If she felt any emotion, it was concealed behind a mask of indifference. Lauren's "hidden agenda" was to discourage interactions at all costs. Lauren developed a thoroughly intransigent avoidance of the adult world. Instead, Lauren learned "maladaptive" ways of coping with her harsh reality. That is, her needs went underground but did not disappear altogether. Her anger and frustration were also submerged.

Lauren brought her expectations about caregivers into her adoptive home. Along with her negative internal working model, she brought her "maladaptive" patterns of behavior and her underground ways of satisfying her needs. Nowhere in her previous life experiences had she learned to deal directly with caregivers about the meeting of her needs, nor had she learned to work out differences of opinion.

In her adoptive placement, Lauren was a skilled thief and a compulsive liar. She believed that she must take (steal) what she needed because it would not be supplied by parental figures. She lied because she perceived that caregivers would be harsh in their punishments if she spoke her true thoughts and feelings.

The literature on the effects and impact of sexual abuse is extensive and demonstrates that the immediate effects of sexual victimization are varied and complex in nature (Browne & Finkelhor, 1986; Kendall-Tackett et al., 1993; Downs, 1993; Nagel, Putman, Noll, & Trickett, 1997). As Ryan writes in Chapter 1, "The potential effects of childhood sexual abuse include a wide array of dysfunctional outcomes for victims during their childhood and as adults. ... Recognition of the many potential negative sequelae of childhood sexual abuse has motivated the demand for and the creation of treatment resources for child victims of sexual abuse." Although dissociation was not originally included in the matrix, group members recognize dissociative responses as a potential outcome and behavioral manifestation in victims of sexual abuse.

These coping mechanisms and behavioral manifestations present a dual dilemma. On the one hand, they are a sign of resiliency, as it is the resilient child who learns to accommodate, to regain a sense of power and control. On the other hand, they are a sign of something unresolved. In her book *The Untouched Key*, Miller (1990) explores clues that are often overlooked in biographies of well-known people, connecting childhood traumas to outcomes in adulthood, from creativity to destructiveness. According to Miller, the shattering effects of traumatic childhood experiences are evident in the biographies of Picasso, Nietzsche, Hitler, and Buster Keaton.

> Although creativity permits survival and helps a person to live with psychic damage, it still conceals rather than reveals the truth. ... Friedrich Nietzsche needed his entire philosophy to shield himself from knowing and telling what really happened to him. Similarly, Buster Keaton learned to be creative without being able to laugh spontaneously. ... They paid a great price for their denial of the truth. (Miller, 1990, pp. 43–44)

"That which does not kill me, makes me stronger," Frankl (1984, p. 103) quoted Nietzsche. Frankl further explained in *Man's Search for Meaning*, "Whatever we had gone through could still be an asset to us in the future" (p. 105). Once the clinician is able to interpret defenses and behaviors as the individual's attempt to overcome feelings of helplessness and powerlessness, it becomes apparent that much of what is described as the pathology of victimization is not initially distorted or dysfunctional, but rather logical and predictable responses used to restore a sense of safety and protection. Without these coping strategies, abuse victims might become psychotic or suicidal.

Yet what is initially adaptive and protective may become dysfunctional over time. This perspective has also been validated by Summit (1983). In "The Child Sexual Abuse Accommodation Syndrome" he describes how the child who experiences abuse learns to accommodate to the situation and to survive. In Summit's words, "There is no way out, no place to run. The healthy, normal resilient child will learn to accommodate to the reality of continuing sexual abuse" (p. 184). Summit also describes the child's struggles and strategies to reconcile and give meaning to the experience of abuse:

> The same mechanisms which allow psychic survival for the child became handicaps to psychological integration as an adult. ... [A]ll these accommodation mechanisms — domestic martyrdom, splitting of reality, altered consciousness, hysterical phenomena, delinquency, sociopathy, projection of rage, and even self-mutilation — are part of the survival skills of the child. (pp. 185–186)

Summit concludes that although the child's immediate coping strategies may be useful, functional, and adaptive in the short term, they may become maladaptive later in life. In order to be healthy, childhood development must remain open to revision based on new input and encourage behavior that elicits supportive responses from others (Ainsworth, 1985). The child's initial adaptation may represent only a temporary solution.

Because we appreciate that the child's abuse is a violation or intrusion, and because clients often experience distressing or problematic symptoms, the literature is likely to overrepresent the negative outcomes of abuse. It has been apparent in the reports of survivors that many suffer the effects of sexual abuse throughout their lives, but it is equally apparent that many go on without becoming symptomatic and do not manifest negative sequelae (Roesler, Riggs, Alareo, & McHorney, 1990).

The clinician's bias is to expect that an experience of sexual abuse will require therapeutic intervention to ameliorate the effects and reduce the risks of dysfunctional outcomes. Yet the therapist's role is not to impose meaning but to discover what meaning is associated with the experience and to make an informed assessment whether the client's understanding and solutions put him/her at risk of further abuse or of becoming abusive to self or others. The process of discovery is discussed in Chapter 5, but that process must be informed by the clinician's awareness of possible symptoms and forethought regarding how clients' coping strategies are likely to generalize over time.

> **It is neither the experience nor the intervention that defines the coping strategy; it is the meaning the child internalizes in his/her contextual view of the world.**

The child who experiences abuse and is able to identify and approach a legitimate caregiver who believes and intervenes to comfort and prevent further abuse may perceive himself/herself as valuable and worthy and conclude that the world is a safe place, even though bad things sometimes happen. Another child may conclude that he/she is helpless and damaged, vulnerable and at risk, and dependent on external sources for protection and control. It is neither the experience nor the intervention that defines the coping strategy; it is the meaning the child internalizes in his/her contextual view of the world.

Not every child requires long-term therapy to ameliorate the effects of abuse. Some arrive at functional solutions on their own, and others access the help they need in the context of other mediating life experiences.

5

The Discovery Process

Jerry Yager, Laurie Knight,
Lynda Arnold, and Ruth Kempe

exual abuse may be the presenting problem that triggers a referral for treatment, or it may be discovered in the history of a
client referred for some other emotional or behavioral problem.
Recognition of a sexual abuse problem may relate to the recent discovery that someone has been abused or abusive or a delayed discovery that someone has a history of victimization or perpetration. The
discovery of the sexual abuse issues may have occurred prior to the
referral because of self-report, or because someone other than the
client either discovered or suspected that sexual victimization had
occurred. Child and adolescent victims are usually encouraged to
seek counseling so that the impact of the abuse can be evaluated, or
they may be brought to counseling for treatment of emotional or
behavioral symptoms. Older survivors of abuse may seek counseling
voluntarily as they recognize that unresolved issues related to their
victimization are continuing to affect their emotional and/or social
functioning. Perpetrators of sexual abuse may be reluctant to seek
counseling voluntarily but are referred or ordered to attend.

Individuals with sexual abuse issues often come into therapy
with similar presenting problems and diagnoses, yet each client has a
unique life history that must be explored and understood in order to
determine a differential diagnosis and provide treatment. Perhaps
because the issue of sexual abuse creates anxiety for therapists as
well as clients, there has been a tremendous temptation to discover a
"recipe" for treating the problems of sexual abuse. Much of the literature on treatment of sexual abuse outlines a constellation of issues
thought to be prevalent among victims and/or perpetrators of sexual

abuse and suggests specific techniques or modules to address these issues. The study group appreciates the utility of structured group work for victims or survivors to counter secrecy and dispel the threats of abusers; to educate victims about the distinctions between healthy sexuality and abuse; and to reassure victims that they are not alone, were right to tell, and are not responsible for the abuse. Similarly, perpetrators of abuse appear to have a constellation of issues in common and benefit from dispelling secrecy and confronting their beliefs that support abusive behavior in a group with peers. These same issues are the basis for many of the community mental health efforts that endeavor to teach the general public about sexual abuse as well as to protect potential victims from being deceived by perpetrators who might approach them. Secrecy has been used as a weapon of abusers and is best dispelled by providing education to groups, whether the group is in a treatment facility, the classroom, the community, or the family.

Such interventions are based on assumptions that do not arise from the client, however, but rather from past experience and research suggesting that most victims have questions relative to these issues. It is imperative to recognize that education or treatment of groups is based on the assumption of sameness: that similar situations are qualitatively the same and, therefore, that persons exposed to similar information or experiences are likely to learn and perceive in a similar fashion. Bennett (1979) describes this assumption of sameness as arising from a sympathetic response. Such sympathy arises from the hearts and heads of well-intentioned persons striving to understand each other by imagining how they would think or feel if they were the other person (perspective taking). In many daily interactions, perspective taking is very effective in understanding experiences and in being able to connect with others through a sympathetic process. The more similar two persons' — or two groups' — experiences, beliefs, and values are, the more effective sympathy is as a basis for understanding (the experience of falling in love is often the result of a powerful sympathetic response, the discovery of sameness).

As Bennett (1979) points out, however, the utility of sympathy breaks down when the experience, beliefs, or values of the other are qualitatively different from those of the sympathizer. In such instances, a higher level of understanding is achieved with the recognition of differentness. The assumption of difference is the basis for

> **The assumption of difference is the basis for empathy, the process of discovering the meaning of experience that is not assumed to be the same as one's own.**

empathy, the process of discovering the meaning of experience that is not assumed to be the same as one's own. Whereas Bennett has applied these concepts to the dilemmas that arise in the cultural diversity of groups, the study group saw a parallel in the developmental diversity and interpersonal diversity of individuals illuminated in the matrix.

While any recipe for treatment is likely to be based on an assumption of sameness, the expertise of specialists is based on a belief that what the "expert" has learned in work with similar cases or clients creates competency. However, the matrix illustrated that one cannot assume developmental or phenomenological similarity on the basis of either a referring symptom or the facts describing a case of sexual abuse. To do so may actually objectify the client in a process paralleling the experience of the abuse itself: disregarding the cues that describe the unique needs, perceptions, and feelings of individual experience. Therapeutic interventions must be based on a process of discovery that validates and personalizes clients' experience, before attempting to intervene to change the way in which they understand or cope with that experience.

The matrix helps to organize the process of searching for and putting together significant pieces of information about individual clients. It also illuminates missing pieces that may be less related to the experience of abuse but of great importance because of their influence on the client's life and current difficulties. This chapter is about the search for the developmental-contextual framework that enables the therapist to reflect an empathic understanding of the significance of the sexual abuse for the client. The study group refers to this therapeutic search as the "process of discovery." The process is first described in terms relevant to older children, adolescents, and adults who are active and verbal partners in the therapeutic process; the implications for younger or less verbal clients are discussed later.

The developmental history of an individual greatly influences how he or she perceives and makes sense of abuse. These perceptions and beliefs profoundly influence subsequent life experiences and directly affect the course of treatment, during which the therapist is evaluating and assigning meaning to the client's behavior. Any assignment of meaning without establishing a developmental-contextual background will be arbitrary. One only has to recall the story of the blind men who incorrectly identified different parts of an elephant because they did not know that the objects they touched were only part of a whole. The therapist's search for a developmental-contextual framework facilitates the discovery of meaning. By knowing the whole client, the meaning of specific features (issues, characteristics, and behaviors) can be understood.

The process of discovering the earlier history of the client and how it may be influencing current functioning is one of the significant variables in facilitating change. In this process, the therapist attempts to create an arena, or space, in which the client can consider his/her past experiences with caregivers, authority figures, dreams, ideals, disappointments, fears, and pleasures. The expectations, perceptions, and internal representations of roles and relationships describe the client's map, which shapes his/her beliefs about the world and can be explored within this arena. The understanding and increased awareness of the client's internalized representation of self, others, and relationships may be one of the most important components of the therapeutic process. The process of discovering the connection between past experiences and present functioning helps the client to view past and present events from a different perspective. By reexamining the past, the client is able to develop alternative interpretations of early life experiences. The questioning of distortions and the validation of feelings that have their roots in the past but live on in the present create the opportunity to alter the frame of reference and broaden the repertoire of cognitive and behavioral coping.

The therapist joins the client in a search for solutions to presenting problems. Past experiences are often the source of intense emotional reactions to current troubles. The therapist teaches the client to examine the current difficulties that prompted him/her to seek treatment and caused the client to feel the need for professional support and guidance. The therapist helps the client not only to verbalize the content of current troubles but also to explore the personal meaning of these life events.

The use of the word "personal" in the previous sentence should be noted. Any conclusions regarding the meaning of events in the lives of our clients outside of their own personal contextual frameworks may appear logical and consistent with a theoretical orientation but may be depersonalizing to the clients and untrue. As Donovan and McIntyre (1990, p. 50) write, "Only by returning human problems to a human context (a context characterized by temporality and relationships), can we begin to discern whether descriptions have truth-value and correspond to fact or whether they are just persuasive appearances." The answer to the question of meaning may be available to the client, or it may be inaccessible. In those cases in which the information that would illuminate the problem of meaning is inaccessible, both the therapist and the client join in a process of searching past memories and forming hypotheses about how the past might be affecting the present. Through the process of discovering the relationship between past experiences and present functioning, a client gains a greater sense of control over his/her choice of responses in the future.

The process of discovering the contextual framework begins as soon as the client makes contact with the therapist, and it continues throughout treatment. It is the interaction between the client and the therapist and the client's experience of that interaction that will either facilitate or block the process of discovery. As the client reveals his/her world within the therapeutic relationship, the therapist uses empathic responses while listening and organizing the data.

Theoretical models can have both a useful function in organizing this information and a problematic function when dealing with the client. On the useful side of the continuum, a model serves as a guide or map when traveling through uncharted psychological territory. Important clinical data are being communicated in what is said as well as in what is not said. A theoretical model assists the therapist in understanding these communications and in developing a framework for interventions to facilitate change. A model can also be helpful in directing the therapeutic search to time periods and events that have been overlooked or avoided. But if the therapist becomes too committed to interpreting clinical data in terms of a model, he/she is at risk of missing important opportunities to learn from the client and to personalize the therapeutic interventions. Inaccurate assessments and ineffective interventions are often the result of a failure to personalize a model — making assumptions rather than searching for hypotheses. The therapist must patiently encourage clients to reveal and express their views of the world without being constrained by a rigid theoretical model.

The matrix presented in Chapter 3 can be a useful model for organizing clinical data. It focuses on developing a comprehensive developmental picture of clients. However, the process of discovering the information and the importance of the data should not be a unilateral process. It should not be a procedure in which the therapist interrogates the client, plugs the information into boxes, and then formulates a conclusion to explain the client's behavior. The process of discovery and the search for the meaning of the connection between a client's current functioning and information from the past are *interactional* processes. The therapist and client make a commitment to work together to identify dysfunctional patterns that at one time in the client's life may have been reasonable or necessary solutions to conflicts or ways of managing overwhelming life experiences but have become problematic in current functioning or pose a risk of future dysfunction.

The matrix was based on the need to understand the larger picture of a client's life in order to make sense of what is currently being observed. Through a process of exploring an individual's early childhood relational experiences, the cognitive and emotional frame of reference prior to the identified abuse experience can be seen. Through the process of taking a history and observing current interactions with the therapist and others, the client and therapist become aware of the links between current situations and past experiences. Many times, current symptoms reflect the client's conscious or unconscious attempts to repeat past experiences in the present as a way of expressing unmet needs or mastering what was uncontrollable in the past.

> **The matrix can serve as a guide for uncovering areas that have been avoided or neglected by the client or the therapist or both in developing the complete picture of the client's life experiences.**

Treatment attempts to distinguish the present from the past, which is currently coloring the present. Some clients experience feelings and thoughts from the past and know that they are incongruent with the present, while others reexperience the overwhelming anxiety from the past and are unable to recognize that their feelings stem from inside. Some clients may believe that the therapist is creating these feelings, just as others did in their past. The clinical intervention must be based on the client's emotional needs, and it must foster developmental growth. The matrix can serve as a guide for uncovering areas that have been avoided or neglected by the client, the therapist, or both in developing a complete picture of the client's life experiences. The client must become aware of what has happened in the past without being overwhelmed by it, understand why what happened in the past is significant and how it influences present relationships, and become able to integrate past and present into a congruent identity. It is within the context of the therapeutic relationship that the client's life puzzle begins to form a picture that reveals the assets and deficits affecting current functioning.

In pursuing an analogy between putting together a puzzle and undertaking the process of discovery, it is helpful to realize that both tasks require a strategic approach to discovering the solution in an efficient, effective manner. When doing a jigsaw puzzle, an individual could attempt to solve the puzzle through trial and error. One could randomly try to fit each piece together until the puzzle was solved. However, by developing a strategy to organize the pieces by similar characteristics, the puzzle solver is able to conserve energy and develop a solution in an economical manner. An individual may begin this task by building a frame from all the edge pieces. However, it is by turning over all the pieces so that the colors and shapes can be observed in relation to one another that the nature of the picture begins to be discerned. The push to organize those pieces reflects a natural discomfort with confusion; the desire to discern the meaning of the picture is driven by curiosity.

Although the matrix provides a useful model to organize the details of a client's life, it is only a frame. Definition of the nature of the phenomena that have shaped and colored the client's developmental path awaits the process of discovery. In the examples presented later in this chapter, the therapists use the matrix as an organizational tool. In the first case, the matrix is used to help the therapist organize the information that the client has presented throughout the course of treatment. In the second case, the therapist actually uses the matrix to help the client organize her own exploration of relevant past history.

Before beginning the discovery process, it is helpful to consider that clients who have experienced the cumulative effect of overwhelming stress throughout childhood tend to develop enduring patterns of responding to anxiety-producing stimuli associated with the original traumatizing event or relationship. To the unconscious, there is no distinction of time. Past events are experienced as occurring in the present. Also, parts of an experience come to represent the whole. Therefore, when any part of a trauma is experienced, it stimulates anxiety, and the unconscious mind prepares for a repetition of the traumatic experience. The therapeutic process tends to generate anxiety for the client that may be perceived as if the client were reexperiencing early childhood traumas. The client's resistance to becoming vulnerable in therapy may be a sign of healthy self-protection. Only when the therapeutic relationship has demonstrated safety and trustworthiness does it become reasonable to invite the client to revisit painful memories.

With a jigsaw puzzle, the strategic approach is to build a frame with the straight-edged pieces before attempting to fit all the internal pieces together. This approach can be compared with the therapist taking the time to create a therapeutic relationship that fosters a sense of safety and security — a frame — before uncovering past internalized traumas. Without this structure to support and contain the intense emotional reactions of the client, a person can be retraumatized by the process of therapy. Therefore, it is the responsibility of the therapist to work with the client on developing a safe, supportive environment in which this exploration can safely take place without overwhelming the client's resources.

As the client and the therapist work to piece together fragmented memories and experiences of the client's life, the shapes of the missing pieces begin to become apparent within the context of the larger picture of the client's whole life experience. What was puzzling to the client before entering treatment (about the way he/she thought about the world and related to others) begins to make sense. The client becomes able to see and understand problems, rather than feeling that he/she *is* the problem.

The following examples are presented to illustrate how the matrix can be used to guide the therapeutic process (see Figures 5.1 and 5.2). Both children were sexually abused, and their responses to the experience were qualitatively different. Understanding the whole life experience of each of these children was necessary to develop effective treatment plans and to understand the children's different responses to the therapeutic process.

EXAMPLE 1:
Nine-year-old Susie was referred by her caseworker to an incest treatment team after disclosing that her adoptive father had molested her from ages 4 through 8. At the time of her referral for treatment, Susie had symptoms of post-traumatic stress disorder (PTSD) thought to be related to the molestation and her witnessing domestic violence between her mother and adoptive father.

Susie's mother called the treatment team to set up therapy for her daughter. The mother believed her daughter's report of the incest and had already separated from the perpetrator prior to disclosure. The mother was concerned that the treatment process be experienced as safe for her daughter and asked the therapist several questions regarding the therapeutic process, the methods used, and the therapist's credentials. She revealed her fear that the therapeutic process might shut her out, given the confidential nature of treatment. She very much wanted to be involved in the process with her daughter in order to rebuild trust and a connection.

Susie's mother described a previously close mother-daughter relationship that had been disrupted after the adoptive father joined the household. She was keenly aware of the importance of security and trust in their relationship as she described her own history of being sexually abused and of being denied support or help by her own mother. As a teenager, the mother recalled riding a bus by herself to see a therapist who had only opened up her pain and offered little healing or guidance for recovery. Later, as an unwed mother, she had made a strong alliance with a caseworker who helped her build functional support systems and take care of Susie as an infant.

As a result of those experiences, the mother was hypervigilant regarding the quality of intervention but had the self-confidence to take the initiative in seeking a safe intervention for her child. The mother also expressed her own guilt for having emotionally abandoned her daughter during the time the incest was occurring. The mother had chosen to work two jobs to avoid her husband because of the severe marital conflict. In this way, she had effectively withdrawn emotionally and physically from her daughter.

The initial contact with the mother, while setting up treatment for Susie, provided valuable information about mother's insight and beliefs regarding personal responsibility; empathy; and the value of trust, safety, and therapeutic intervention and her hope for healing to occur in the mother-daughter relationship. These values and attitudes gave the therapist useful information to form preliminary hypotheses about Susie's early life experiences and her care by the mother, although these assumptions needed further scrutiny.

In the first meetings with Susie and her mother, the therapist noted how articulate both mother and daughter were and that they volunteered pertinent information. The mother revealed that she had given birth to Susie as an unwed teenager, living in an extended family setting with her disabled mother. (Susie and her mother were once again living in this home.) Susie was described as a good baby, easy to care for. The mother had received help from Social Services to enhance her parenting skills. Both mother and daughter spoke of the birth father as avoiding responsibility for Susie and ultimately abandoning her. Both also described communication problems in the family and frequent conflicts between Susie and her mother. They both presented information describing an enmeshed, chaotic extended family with patterns of role reversal. Defense mechanisms consisted of denial, avoidance, and rationalization.

Susie's childhood was initially full of support systems until the adoptive father's arrival, when economic stress, isolation, and domestic violence became problems. As the therapist explored the past and present with Susie and her mother, it became clear that Susie had received good care within a relatively safe and supportive environment prior to the mother's marriage to the adoptive father when Susie was 4 years old. Additionally, Susie was a bright, verbal, attractive child with the capacity for empathy, trust, insight, and independence. By exploring Susie's life prior to the onset of abuse, the therapist was able to assess Susie's resources, developmentally as well as within her family and community. This exploration gave the therapist insight about how Susie might have perceived her sexual abuse. Together, Susie and the therapist continued in their process of discovery.

Being victimized was incongruent with Susie's prior life experiences. She had developed a sense of basic trust in a secure relationship with her mother. She had shown the ability to be autonomous and to achieve developmental milestones. At age 4, Susie suddenly found herself alone, betrayed, violated, helpless, and afraid. She believed that reporting the abuse would endanger her mother's life and her own survival, so she remained silent and felt trapped.

Susie was at a stage of development where she should have been playing, socializing with friends, and figuring out what it means to be a little girl. Instead, she became isolated, depressed, unsure of herself, and insecure in her world. She began developing cognitive distortions to accommodate her experience. Sadly, she decided that being a girl was undesirable. She decided to be a tomboy, convincing herself that being boyish would make her "tough" and give her power to protect herself. She disowned her femininity and became in many ways alienated from herself. She developed a poor self-image.

Figure 5.1 Sexual Abuse in the Context of Whole Life Experience: Susie, Age 10

		Temperament: Extrovert/interactive; determined/persistent; clear boundaries/signals; easy to comfort	**Physical:** Attractive; no health problems		**Neurological:** None	
CONDITION AT BIRTH	endow-ment	**Parental expectations:** Wanted girl Viewed as "cute" Easy to mother, care for "Good baby"	**Coping styles:** Closed communication Used drugs, alcohol, & work to avoid conflict Also used constructive resources outside family to adapt	**Characteristics:** Enmeshed (with extended family) Chaotic Loose boundaries Role reversal Birth father never involved (teen parents)	**Defense mechanisms:** Distortion Denial/avoidance Rationalization (very intelligent, good at intellectualizing)	**Environment:** Domestic violence (after 4 yrs old). Support systems. Economic stress. Conflict of sexual attitudes. Difficulty with marital intimacy and disruption in mother/child bond when "Susie" was 4 years old
HISTORY	family of origin					
		Empathic care: Trust Confident	**Neglectful care:** None	**Learning styles:** Opportunity Intelligent Experiential	**Physical abuse:** None	**Emotional abuse:** None	**Substance Abuse:** Mother used on occasion. Utilized a sister and good/consistent day care for when she used (not extended periods)	**Parental loss:** Depression (compensated by utilizing sister and baby-sitter)	**Rejection:** Abandoned by birth father — he was never involved (teen parent)	**Trauma:** None
	early childhood experience prior to sexual abuse*									
EXPERIENCE OF SEXUAL ABUSE		**Sexual humiliation or trauma**	**Hands off:** Peep, flash, obscenity	**Hands on:** Fondling, genital stimulation	**Observation:** Pornography: had to view movies	**Penetration:** Attempted intercourse	**Genital injury:** None
		Age/Developmental Stage: 4–8 years old, gender identity, role confusion					
		Relationship of abuser: Adoptive Father					
		Child's perception of relationship:	He was supposed to love and protect, but instead he trapped and tortured her. Felt he hated her.	He was authoritative and she and her family were dependent on him and feared him.	She trusted him briefly, then developed profound mistrust.		

*Prior to age 4; sexual abuse began immediately after marriage occurred.

Figure 5.1 Sexual Abuse in the Context of Whole Life Experience: Susie, Age 10 (cont.)

EXPERIENCE OF SEXUAL ABUSE (cont.)	**Duration:** Chronic for 4 years				
	Method of engagement: Force, violence, perceived threat to mother's family's safety due to domestic violence.				
	Child's perception:	**Cognitive:** Believed normal way fathers treated kids then felt hated by him, that she was bad	**Physical:** Pain, arousal	**Emotional:** Fear, helpless, alone, anxious, rare but occasional pleasure, felt "trapped in a chamber of rotten things."	**Secondary gains:** Believed was getting some attention
DISCLOSURE	**Delayed:** Delayed until parents separated				
	Effective intervention				
	Consequences of disclosure:	**Victim:** Relieved, felt believed and protected. Initially some shame that reality of experience known. Ambivalence over wish for father to be punished. Occasional fear he'd retaliate for disclosure		**Family:** Breakup of family. Mother enraged at husband who she has now divorced. Youngest children miss their father, but also feel relieved he's gone. Misses his extended family.	**Offender:** Admitted with minimization; sentenced to prison but released on appeal/bond.
OUTCOMES	**Issues:** Anxiety; humiliation; lack of control; helplessness, vulnerability, powerlessness; embarrassment, shame, guilt, betrayed; devalued; post-traumatic stress disorder; loss; confusion: sexual, cognitive, role, boundary, relationships	**Characteristics:** Poor self-image, lack of trust (males), rejection, personalizing sexual offense, depression, preoccupation with chronic triggers causing reliving of experience and feelings, sadness. (Initially in treatment, conflict with mother was primary concern.)		**Manifestations:** Some power/control behaviors, withdrawal, post-traumatic stress disorder; aggression, thoughts of self-destructive behavior. Gender identity confusion, wish to be a tomboy to be "tough" and able to take care of self.	
	Predictions for Subsequent Life Experiences: Struggles with: depression, hyposexuality, feminine identity, intimacy within relationships with males				

Laurie Knight, 1993

Susie benefited from her mother's help and direct involvement in the therapy process, which reestablished a secure base from which to venture onward in the discovery process and to help Susie catch up developmentally. Because of Susie's developmental history, it was clear that the therapeutic relationship should not be paramount for Susie in her recovery process, but rather that she and her mother needed to be reconnected. The therapist's role was to guide the two of them through that process.

Just as Susie's mother had brought her own matrix into play in her involvement with Susie and the therapy, the therapist's matrix influenced an oversight in Susie's process of discovery. Early in treatment, Susie volunteered statements about her birth father's "golden eyes," like hers, and said, "At least I know his name." The significance of Susie's abandonment by her birth father slipped by the therapist, who had herself experienced a degree of abandonment by her father. The therapist focused instead on the adoptive father and his abuse of Susie. However, the birth father's abandonment was critical to Susie's perception of the abuse and greatly influenced the meaning of the abuse.

A review of the matrix helped the therapist recognize her own blind spot and allowed for a refocus in the therapeutic process. As the focus shifted back to Susie's abandonment by her birth father and what it meant to her, it became clear that the abandonment was closely tied to the devastation of the abuse. The birth father's abandonment potentiated the effects of her sexual abuse, in that during the abuse, Susie's fantasy was of being rescued by her birth father. Of course, he never came, and every time she was abused, she reexperienced abandonment (by both parents), feeling alone, empty, and worthless. Therapeutic work needed to focus on Susie's grief over the loss of her birth father and to challenge the cognitive distortions she developed because she was abandoned. Her emptiness within herself needed to be explored, her losses grieved, and a more powerful feminine self constructed.

> Had the therapist stayed on the course of focusing on the sexual abuse and PTSD symptoms, she would have missed a critical piece in Susie's healing process.

Had the therapist continued focusing on the sexual abuse and PTSD symptoms, she would have missed a critical piece in Susie's healing process. The development of a whole self for Susie required an understanding of her whole life experience and how her developmental history shaped her worldview and how the experience of the sexual abuse affected her. For Susie, the sexual abuse was like being held "hostage in a chamber of rotten stuff," unworthy of rescue by her birth father, and invisible to her mother. For her, it was a living "hell."

Susie was fortunate in that she had a good enough life experience prior to the sexual abuse to allow her to develop basic trust and the desire and capacity for achievement and autonomy. She was born with the advantages of being above average in intelligence, physically attractive, and healthy, with a pleasant disposition. She was able to reconnect with her mother and develop a solid therapeutic alliance. She became aware of her resources and expanded them, while she was learning to use them. She had a positive experience in therapy and knows that she can return to work on a more positive feminine self-image, when she is ready, and to process further her losses and trauma if she becomes depressed again. Susie's prognosis for a positive future is hopeful.

EXAMPLE 2:
Eight-year-old Donna exemplifies a very different contextual matrix. She was referred to treatment by her Social Services caseworker because she had been sexually abused by her father and adolescent brother.

In the initial session, Donna made no eye contact, verbalized little, and showed a flat affect. In the play therapy room, she did little to explore the environment. The therapist found it very difficult to make a connection with Donna. During her interview, Donna's mother spent most of the time talking about her own childhood and how she had been abandoned to fend for herself. Both mother and child were reluctant to discuss the sexual abuse, and the mother had indicated to other professionals that she didn't believe that either Donna or her 10-year-old brother had really been sexually abused by her husband. Donna's mother had testified in defense of her husband at his criminal trial. At the time of the intake, Donna's father was serving time in prison for sexual assault on Donna's brother. An older brother was in a residential treatment facility because of his sexual perpetration against her, which he denied.

Donna's treatment was sporadic and unpredictable, as her mother would forget her appointments. Within three months, Donna and two siblings were placed in foster care when Donna's brother alleged that their mom's new boyfriend had been physically and sexually abusive. Donna denied these allegations and was very angry at her brother for reporting.

Since the mother was unable to give an accurate family history, the therapist used the matrix to guide the search for information. Social Services records revealed a history of a very chaotic family lifestyle prior to the sexual abuse. Domestic violence was prevalent, including one incident when the father tried to stab the mother while she was pregnant with Donna. Soon after Donna's birth, Donna and her mother were hit by a car. The record did not reveal what (if any) physical trauma Donna sustained, but it was safe to imagine that Donna's earliest life experiences had not been conducive to perceptions of safety and protection.

Donna reported that she remembered being sexually abused by a stranger at age 3, in the alley near her home. She believed that her mother had called the police. No record of the incident was found, but Donna's memory was sufficient to suggest a continued lack of protection. The sexual abuse by her father started when Donna's mother went to work. The history did not reveal any support systems in the father's family, and according to Donna, "My dad's mom hates my mom." Donna's mom had no family, as she had been abandoned at an early age. Reviewing the history, it appeared that nothing in Donna's life had ever been predictable or trustworthy.

After Donna's placement in foster care, her treatment became more consistent and predictable. Donna continued to avoid any discussion of her abuse and was disconnected and isolating. Finally, the therapist realized that this child had never developed beyond the trust versus mistrust stage, and the intervention changed. Food was provided as a sign of nurturance to facilitate the development of trust, and therapy was purposely scheduled for the same time and day each week. Donna was provided with a safe environment for play therapy, with lots of choices to feel independent and competent. Donna came to expect snacks and to ask for specific foods. She also began to question the therapist's memory of previous sessions to see if the relationship was valued enough to be remembered and to compare her perceptions with those of the therapist. Many hours were spent playing games, with Donna always feeling that she needed to cheat to win. As in her life, manipulation was a survival skill. Eventually she made a choice to learn to play fair so that she could use this new skill to make friends outside play therapy. Donna also began to initiate and test the limits of the therapeutic relationship.

During this time, Donna's mother became pregnant by the boyfriend who had allegedly abused Donna and her siblings. The mother withdrew from any involvement with her children and virtually disappeared. Donna's view of this situation was self-blame and a belief that she didn't deserve her mother's attention or concern. However, based on the trust that had developed in the therapeutic relationship, Donna became able to express her anger and sadness over her abandonment by her mom.

The matrix was used with Donna on several occasions to help her create a "life line" of her history. This gave Donna a concrete (distancing) way to look at her life. The matrix also allowed Donna to gently confront some of her cognitive distortions and realize why she had needed defense mechanisms (such as denial) to survive in her family. Donna initially identified that her life had happened in this way "because I deserve it." This revelation allowed the therapy to explore feelings of helplessness and depression. She was evaluated for depression and was prescribed medication that enabled her to experience and process her feelings without being overwhelmed and to control her angry outbursts.

It was only after this process that she could work on the sexual abuse by her father and how he had used a gun to threaten her into silence about it, as well as her fear that he would harm other people in the family. This fear was realistic, based on the history of domestic violence. To Donna, the sexual abuse was just one more event in her life that validated her view that neither the outside world nor her family were trustworthy and that she did not deserve good things happening to her. Even now, in foster care and therapy, it was reasonable that she would distrust nurturance. The connection was made that her mother's going to work had left her even more vulnerable to be molested and intensified the feelings of abandonment.

As Donna began to trust her new environment, particularly her foster parents, she began to act out more. In some ways, this was a positive sign. She became more verbal and made more eye contact. Donna was also doing better at school and extended her trust to a female teacher. Limit-setting in the foster home continued to trigger feelings of inadequacy, power and control issues, and fear of abandonment. However, the structure also allowed Donna to feel safe and was a very important container for the vulnerable self she was beginning to get in touch with. The foster parents were included in part of the treatment strategies so that Donna could be encouraged to express her feelings in current situations and experience a sense of validation from the foster parents.

Eventually, Donna's father was released from prison and returned to the community, planning to resume custody of Donna and her brothers. The mother was still absent. Additional work on the sexual abuse was necessary because the father was still denying that he had molested. A real dilemma occurred for Donna because she had no other family resources; in her mind, her only hope was to idealize her relationship with her father. Denial of the sexual abuse became the only viable option, which she took. However, although Donna was able to say that she wanted to see her dad, she was also able to say that she didn't want to live with him. As this dilemma brought family issues back to the forefront of treatment, the abandonment by Donna's mother needed additional work in treatment as well.

At age 11, Donna continues to struggle with low self-esteem and the desire to belong. Puberty has triggered feelings of vulnerability related to being female, and she is also struggling with cultural issues related to growing up Hispanic in a mainstream Anglo culture. Donna has remained in the same foster home, and the court has considered it a permanent placement. However, the foster parents are older and

Figure 5.2 Sexual Abuse in the Context of Whole Life Experience: Donna

CONDITION AT BIRTH (endowment, family of origin)

Temperament: Introvert/avoidant	Physical: Low birth weight		Neurological: None	
Parental expectations: Mother liked daughter. To give back to mom	Coping styles: Closed communications. Alcohol used by father. Work used to avoid marital conflict	Characteristics: Enmeshed. Chaotic. Loose boundaries. Hispanic	Defense mechanisms: Distortions. Denial/avoidance. Repression. Idealization	Environment: Economic stress, no support systems, sexual attitudes, attachment problems, marital stress, parental violence

HISTORY (early childhood experience prior to sexual abuse)

Empathic care: Father—no. Mother—no	Neglectful care: Yes—due to chaotic environment. Didn't follow through with therapy—dirty clothes, didn't teach self-care.	Learning styles: Impoverished environment, lower I.Q., lacking cognitive stimulation	Physical abuse: Probably physical abuse—mom and siblings	Emotional abuse: Confusion	Substance Abuse: Father	Parental loss: Abandonment by father. Depression of mother.	Rejection: ??	Trauma: Physical abuse by dad during mom's pregnancy. Car accident. Neglect.

EXPERIENCE OF SEXUAL ABUSE

Sexual humiliation or trauma	Hands off: None	Observation: Sexual abuse of others	Hands on: Fondling, genital stimulation	Penetration: Vaginal and anal	Genital injury: None

Age/Developmental Stage:

Relationship of abuser: Stranger, sibling, father

Child's perception of relationship:

Roles/Expectations: Authority, distrust

Figure 5.2 Sexual Abuse in the Context of Whole Life Experience: Donna (cont.)

EXPERIENCE OF SEXUAL ABUSE (cont.)

Duration: One-time rape. Repetitive by sibling and father.

Method of engagement: Bribes, lures. Coercion ("had gun"). Threat and loss ("Mom will leave you"). Threats ("threatened to kill me").

Child's perception:

Cognitive:	Physical:	Emotional:	Secondary gains:
"I'm getting punished for being bad."	Painful	Fear, anxiety	Attention, money, going places, appeasing Dad to reduce violence

DISCLOSURE

Delayed: When brother placed, other children disclosed.

Intervention: Ineffective, originally not placed. Treatment focus only on sexual abuse.

Consequences of disclosure:

Victim:	Family:	Offender:
Fear, shame, guilt, blame, loss of family	Break-up, loss of members, denial/minimization	Denial, personal threats, loss — went to prison

OUTCOMES

Issues:	Characteristics:	Manifestations:
Anxiety, humiliation, lack of control, helplessness, vulnerability, powerlessness, embarrassment, shame, guilt, betrayal, devalued, post-traumatic stress, loss, confusion, sexual and cognitive role boundary, relationships	Poor self-image, lack of trust, distorted thinking, negative expectations, rejection, failure, blames self, depression, fear of intimacy, sadness	Setting self up for rejection, power/control, withdrawal, isolating, post-traumatic stress disorder, thinking errors, somatic complaints, attention deficit disorder, learning disability, poor hygiene, revictimization

Predictions for Subsequent Life Experiences: Depression/suicide, runaway, domestic violence relationship, drugs, alcohol, teen pregnancy

Lynda Arnold, 1993

have some fears regarding their ability to raise Donna and her brothers in the long term.

A change in therapists was precipitated by changes in program guidelines. Donna felt that the change was due to her being bad. This time she was able to demonstrate these feelings more directly rather than by totally isolating herself. The termination process became extremely important so that Donna could have a "normal" experience of beginning and ending a relationship.

Donna is likely to continue to have characterological problems due to the poor attachment during early life; she is likely to continue to struggle with relationships in the future. However, based on the discovery journey with her therapist, she has learned that she is deserving and capable of good things and that there are trustworthy people.

In summary, the process of discovery for Susie and Donna, referred for treatment with the same presenting problem, was very different, even though they shared some common issues. All clients, whether younger or older, victims or perpetrators, can benefit from the experience of piecing together their lifelines and integrating experiences into a coherent sense of self. The following case study demonstrates a similar process of discovery that differentiates the phenomenology of two siblings who developed abusive behaviors very early in life.

EXAMPLE 3:

"Bro" and "Sis" were born into a large family in rural Colorado in which multigenerational incest had taken place. There were five older siblings (three male, two female) ages 8 to 17. The grandfather was incarcerated and the father was on probation due to incest in the home.

When Bro was 5 and Sis was 3, Bro was hospitalized for a week with anal lacerations and severe gonorrhea. Social Services determined that both Bro and Sis had been sexually abused by the older brothers and that Bro had also been sexually abusive to Sis with instruction and encouragement from the siblings. Both children were removed from the home, and parental rights were terminated. Foster care records identified Sis as a "victim" and Bro as a "perpetrator."

Bro was placed in an extremely abusive foster home with many other children who were beaten, locked up, not fed, and verbally denigrated by the foster parents. "They beat us for things a parent shouldn't," Bro recalled later, such as for eating apples off the tree in the yard. The foster father was a sheriff, and the foster mother referred to Bro as "a perpetrator and a liar." Bro was sodomized repeatedly by an older foster child, but no one believed his outcries.

Sis went to a different foster home, but the placement was soon disrupted "due to emotional and behavioral disturbance," according to Social Services records. "It didn't last long because I had learned the abusive ways, you know," she said later, recounting her sexual behaviors with her foster siblings. When Sis was removed from the foster home, she was hospitalized and received several months of intensive psychiatric treatment. By age 5, she was placed in a long-term residential treatment setting.

One year later, Bro was finally removed from the foster home when another child reported the abusive conditions and was believed. Bro was 8 years old and lived in his next foster home for about two years until he sexually abused the foster mother's granddaughter. Bro never denied his behaviors with his sister or in the foster home, but he said later, "I don't hold myself accountable for that behavior as offending. It was just the way I was taught to behave."

He was placed in a residential center at age 11 and was very disruptive and noncompliant. He sexually assaulted a younger girl while on a pass and later remembered, "Now that was an offense. I knew I was angry!" Now on probation, he spent the next year in a locked psychiatric setting where he was forced to attend group treatment with older adolescents and adult sexual offenders. In that group he was put on the "hotseat" while other group members confronted him, calling him a "baby raper."

At age 13, Bro was moved to an unlocked adolescent psychiatric unit where, he remembers, "I finally got some help there from one guy." That same year, Sis (who was now 11) graduated from the residential facility to a group home and was doing well with school and peers.

One year later, Bro was placed in long-term residential care and referred to an "offense-specific" group. He was happy about the residential program but initially was adamant in resisting the offense-specific group. Now age 15, he described himself and his life entirely in terms of abuse: victimization and perpetration were his whole identity.

About two years later, Sis (not quite 14) was discharged to live with an older sister who was doing very well. Both Bro and Sis had maintained contact with this older sister, and since it seemed apparent that she would now bring Sis into occasional contact with Bro, a joint therapy session was arranged. In observation of that reunion, therapists noticed that the striking similarity of these siblings' early experience was in vivid contrast to the disparity of the system's response to them and their subsequent case management and treatment:

- Bro's earliest behaviors had resulted in labeling him a perpetrator, although he had clearly been abused as well.
- Very similar behaviors by Sis triggered intense, long-term treatment focused on her victimization.

- Bro was in custodial care for six years before a treatment referral was made, and that was focused on his perpetration. His course of treatment lasted eight years: two years in a hospital, five years in two residential treatment programs, and one year in a community-based emancipation program.
- Sis was referred for treatment within months of placement in custodial care. Her course of treatment lasted 11 years: less than one year in a hospital, six years in residential treatment, and four years in a community-based group home.

Sis left the system at age 14, and was reunited with the one "survivor" of the family. In follow-up, Sis did well at home and in school, graduating from high school and going on to community college. Bro left the system at age 19, emancipated and alone but having graduated from high school and registered for community college. In follow-up reports, it was learned that he had dropped out of college to return to his hometown. In exploring his relationship to his older brothers, he engaged in some high-risk behaviors. By age 22, however, he had a job and an apartment and was attending the local community college.

One of the treatment goals for this boy had been for him to integrate his history of victimization and perpetration into a more diverse identity: to recognize the risk of abuse in the future, but not define his whole identity in those terms. He was a gentle young man, musically talented and good-natured, who thought that he might do well and be a counselor. But in his own words, "I won't ever have kids or work with them — just too high-risk for me after all that's happened."

Other authors, such as Hindman (1989) have presented formalized processes that can be useful for gathering data with older clients. Some suggestions on how to gather data to illuminate the discovery process in a less formalized way are listed below:

- Pay attention to who initiates the referral process for therapy. Who is asking for intervention? Whose problem is it?

- Listen to what is being said, what is not being said, and how information is revealed within the context of the relationship.

- Use open-ended questions to allow the client to interject his/her perceptions rather than responding to an assumption (e.g., "You tell me that your brother does bad things to you. Can you tell me more about what he does that feels bad?" rather than "Is he touching you in a sexual way?" which arises from the assumption that the sexual abuse of record is what was perceived as bad).

- Read collateral reports and speak with significant people in the client's life in order to gather additional information about life history: is there a grandmother, neighbor, or teacher who knows the child well? Reviewing old case files or family albums, if available, may be useful.

- Experience how it feels to be in the room with the client. Is he/she open, trusting, and vulnerable, or closed, resistant, and oppositional? What are the affective and verbal clues? What is the client projecting onto the therapist in the current relationship?

- Observe patterns of behavior. Does the client keep appointments regularly? Is the client always late or early? Does he/she take a coat off or leave it on? How close or far away does he/she sit? What are the nonverbal clues?

Treatment of younger clients requires the therapist to use a variety of therapeutic techniques to access the meaning and impact of abuse on the client's life. These techniques may also be used with older, less verbal clients. The less the verbal response or input from the client, the greater the pull for the therapist to project his or her own interpretation of the event onto the client's experience. Yet we cannot assume that the sexual abuse was traumatic. People react to sexualized experiences differently. Accurate empathy requires the therapist to read the cues of the child and to respond to the child's needs rather than to his/her own needs.

Through interviews with the child's parents or guardians, information related to the child and the environmental conditions at the time of birth can provide a picture of the child's functioning prior to the abuse. Observations of the child with caregivers can highlight the quality of the child's attachment and the ability of the parent to empathically respond to the child. Part of this assessment is to monitor the family's capacity to create a safe environment for a victim and contain the impulses of a perpetrator. If other professionals are involved, coordination of services increases the likelihood that services will be offered in an effective manner. Through some form of play therapy, the therapist can piece together the child's phenomenological experience of the abuse.

Lenore Terr's (1990a, 1990b) research suggests that the worst thing that can be done is to put off treatment. Children may appear nonsymptomatic, yet they may have been greatly affected by their experience.

EXAMPLE 4:
Six-year-old Jane was involved in treatment not because she had been abused but because her 11-year-old brother had been violently sexually abused by their stepfather. Jane was doing well in school and was not exhibiting problematic symptoms. During a family session, the therapist asked Jane what she does to have fun at home. Jane reported that she plays house in her room. In response to further questions, Jane reported that there is always an ambulance parked right below the little girl's window in case somebody gets hurt. The therapist reported that neither Jane nor anyone else in the family felt that the play scenario was related to her past experience. The parents thought that the therapist was overinterpreting her play. Jane's mother also felt that if they could only be back together as a family and forget the past everything would be all right again. The trauma had clearly affected the little girl's worldview. How her altered worldview will influence her future development is yet to be determined.

Successful treatment is facilitated when the therapist is prepared to enter the client's world and guide him/her on a journey through the client's own life experiences, uncovering the meaning that the experiences have for the client and how these meanings are influencing current functioning and the quality of life. It is the wise therapist who can tolerate the uncertainty of not knowing the meaning while relying on teamwork with the client to discover it. This process is an adventure for both client and therapist as both come to understand their own unique differences and similarities as human beings who are faced with difficult life experiences.

The developmental status of young children enforces different priorities in evaluation and treatment. It changes and often limits their capacity to respond in an evaluation and history-taking process, necessitating the use of other historians and records to supplement and corroborate the child's story. The preschool child's understanding and use of language may mislead the unwary interviewer; concrete language, differences in perception of such elements as time, and thought processes that do not include deductive reasoning can make for confusion in interpreting a child's responses. With young children especially, a therapist must be careful about relying solely on verbal statements, particularly if they have been obtained by a leading or intimidating mode of questioning.

In the beginning, an emphasis on clarity and reliability — the therapist doing what he/she says he/she will — and an awareness of the importance to the child of feeling safe and not alienated from caregivers are realistic goals. Shorter sessions with establishment of a comfortable rapport are usually more productive than longer sessions that overtax a child's attention span.

Because children are generally more action oriented and abused children may be less skillful in some verbal abilities, play activities are usually an important part of evaluation and treatment. Drawing, dollhouse play, animal families, and puppets all encourage activity and expression of feelings. Children often reenact in play the kind of everyday activities they know, although sometimes in exaggerated form. Sometimes word games, storytelling, and sentence-completion games are helpful as supports for older or nonverbal children in describing their feelings.

> **Successful treatment is facilitated when the therapist is prepared to enter the client's world and guide him/her on a journey through the client's own life experiences.**

Observation of nonverbal cues or repetitive behavior can provide very important clues. Verbalization of the observations or simple responsiveness to them can further establish rapport and understanding.

The therapist needs to be sure that the child understands generally why the meeting is taking place, and the family needs to give permission to the child to talk freely. Seeing a young child and his or her family together for clarification of the treatment process and then separately for privacy of disclosures is usually reassuring to a child who is concerned about his/her parents' approval. In both assessment and treatment, the child's dependent status can never be forgotten. Most of all, any child needs his/her parents' care and love; their disapproval of participation in treatment may be threatening and make it impossible for the child to make use of the freedom of expression that treatment offers. Even when the attachment bond has been broken and the child is in placement, with little open acknowledgment of abusive behavior at home, many children wish to maintain the only attachment they have known and return to an abusive environment.

All therapeutic work must be done through the medium of the relationship between therapist and client. With children, the relationship the therapist offers may become very important over time, as what the therapist can offer in terms of safety, trustworthiness, and empathy becomes more apparent.

6

Therapeutic Intervention as Mediation of Subsequent Life Experience

Tim Fuente and Sherri Wand

I f one thinks of therapy as a journey through uncharted psychological territory, the matrix we are presenting may serve as the map and compass. That is, it may be used to give the therapist and the client a sense of direction based on where the client has been as well as where the client wants to go.

The matrix helps the therapist and the client to step back from the symptom of the moment and view the big picture of a whole life's experience. This contextual view suggests that therapy consider (1) what the client brings with him/her, (2) the setting into which the client comes, (3) what surrounds the client, and (4) how the client interacts within the environment along the developmental path. Within this matrix, the action of one's life is played out. The dynamics of one's life are the shapes and shades and colors of relationships and events that define the topography and terrain of the map. The most relevant aspect of those dynamics is one's perception. The interpretation and meanings the individual attaches to relationships and events become part of the foundation for subsequent functioning. It is that foundation that is explored and altered by treatment in order to moderate negative outcomes in subsequent life experience.

It is imperative that therapy assist the client in understanding his/her own meanings for these events. In order to do this, the work must be contained and managed within a cognitive framework. This framework becomes a type of vessel that holds the therapeutic relationship and combines the client's developmental and contextual structures. The trauma perspective, attachment perspective, and other specific theoretical perspectives can further enhance understanding.

Within this framework, client and therapist identify treatment goals relevant to the very real problems and issues that the client experiences. When the client is a child or other person with limited verbal skills, caregivers may help to articulate the current problems, or the child may show the issues in play.

> **It is imperative that therapy assist the client in understanding his/her own meanings for these events.**

Treatment is a process of setting goals and providing interventions that bring relevance to everything that has been discovered. The therapeutic process and the therapeutic relationship are imperative components that must encompass an intervention designed to achieve specific as well as general treatment goals. Client and therapist must develop an informed strategy to achieve these goals and must identify what part the relationship plays and how it can be used to meet these goals. Treatment planning needs to consider both past and present client relationships, individual competency with respect to resistance and capacity, potential risks and assets (Gilgun, 1996), and directions for growth.

A variety of treatment modalities and treatment techniques are useful when they are anchored in a solid therapeutic process. Research has confirmed that the presence of such qualities as positive regard, genuineness, empathy, and caring within the alliance enhances the effectiveness of any treatment modality.

For some clients, the experience of sexual abuse is one of the more powerful events in life. For others, an experience of sexual abuse is yet one more hill or mud hole along an arduous path. It is important for a therapist treating a client who was sexually abused and/or abusive to understand that person's interpretation of the abuse. This process redirects the focus from the facts of the event itself to the uniquely personal experience of the event. Too often therapists look at the nature and characteristics of victimization or perpetration to determine a therapeutic plan for intervention. The relevance of abuse is in the assimilation and accommodation of abuse into the context of the individual's whole life.

When the experience of sexual abuse is viewed in the context of prior and subsequent life experiences and the meanings attached to them, therapeutic intervention can be specifically tailored for that individual. The client's attempts to understand and adapt to the abuse emerge as therapeutic issues, that is, the way these dynamics are brought into the present. The nature and direction of therapeutic interventions should be defined by the phenomenology of the client's life. The variables related to the individual, the family, and prior life experiences may be more relevant to the client's adaptation to abuse experiences than the particulars of the abuse itself.

The research suggests that child victims' immediate accommodation is profoundly affected by the context surrounding them. Children who are able to tell and who receive supportive validation at the time of the abuse appear to be more likely to accommodate and assimilate the abuse without internalizing responsibility. They seem less likely to accept the blame or stigma of abuse as defining something about themselves and are more likely to place the responsibility with the perpetrator. Yet it cannot be assumed that it is the act of telling or the experience of supportive validation that rejects abuse in the child's developmental progression; the child was able to tell only because of the context of his/her prior life experience. The child who tells brought into the experience beliefs of worthiness and the expectation of receiving validation of this experience from caregivers. In the phenomenology of the child who tells is the view that others will react to expressions of distress by intervening to meet the child's needs. The child is able to reject the perpetrator's view of the world as dissonant with his/her own experience; the child rejects the perpetrator's attempts to attribute responsibility to the child and does not believe any threats attempting to discount the efficacy of the child's own secure base.

Yet we can understand, too, that abuse may be so traumatic that it overwhelms even the secure child's prior beliefs or that children who do tell and receive support and protection may nonetheless be affected by distortions that negatively shape their subsequent assimilation. These issues were raised in Ryan's original victim-to-victimizer article (see Chapter 1). The therapeutic intervention must not be based on assumptions about the experience of abuse or about the presenting symptom (or lack of apparent symptoms) that narrow the therapist's scope of exploration. The process of discovery detailed in Chapter 5 must be informed by questions, not conclusions.

In order to understand the client's unique adaptation to abuse, the therapist must understand the client's development and beliefs about self, others, and the world and the client's interaction with each. This focus illuminates the importance of the client's attachments to the significant people in his/her life and a sense of competence in coping with life experiences. As mentioned in Chapter 3, experiences of attachment form the foundation for subsequent beliefs and behaviors. Exploration of the phenomenology or worldview of the individual reveals numerous hypotheses regarding the nature of past and present relationships as well as developmental competence.

Treatment Goals and Objectives

Simply stated, the goal of any psychotherapy is to enable clients to integrate their responses to life experiences in a way that reduces the risk of distortions and symptoms, improves functioning, and prevents long-term dysfunction. These goals are no different when the client is a child dealing with physical or verbal abuse at the hands of parents or peers, an adolescent dealing with issues of parental conflicts related to separation anxieties, or an adult dealing with marital discord or midlife uncertainties. Yet the practice of treating sexual abuse issues across the life span has been viewed as a specialty, somehow inherently different from other therapeutic challenges.

At first glance, it might appear that the thing that makes sexual abuse different and requires extra training for the therapist is its sexual aspects. Indeed, the vast majority of professionals in the therapeutic community have had little, if any, meaningful training in human sexuality. Sexology is viewed as a specialty in counseling professions throughout the world. Many counselors experience the same discomfort in discussing sexual issues with clients as do parents with their children. Sexuality is viewed as so personal and so private that discussing it openly may feel voyeuristic or intrusive to either or both of the parties.

EXAMPLE 1:
One member of the study group was troubled by a 7-year-old boy who was reporting a chronic preoccupation with masturbation. The therapist recognized the compensatory nature of this behavior yet was

uncertain how to address the risk of it becoming a cycle of sexual dysfunction. He had worked with the boy in processing the early parts of the cycle related to his tendency to isolate and knew that the boy frequently engaged in masturbatory behavior while isolating. Yet the therapist was reticent to inquire about the fantasies associated with the behavior because the behavior was occurring in private and he was unsure if he would be "intruding" or violating the boy's privacy boundaries if he asked about the fantasies.

With encouragement from the group, he rallied the courage to ask, "What do you think about when you masturbate?" Without any hesitation, the child described in detail his memory of the violent, intrusive assaults he had experienced and connected the masturbation to the physical arousal he experienced whenever this memory unfolded in his mind. The therapist's simple question revealed both a classic post-traumatic stress disorder (PTSD) symptom (recurring memory associated with a ritualized behavior) and a high risk for reinforcement of the aggression-arousal connection.

In this example, sexuality had been significantly affected, and intervention was clearly required. However, in many cases the sexual aspect may be less important in defining what is "different" in sexual abuse counseling than another aspect: the abuse of trust. Early in the Kempe Center's work with incest families (Kempe & Kempe, 1984; Mrazek & Kempe, 1981), an unpublished paper titled "The Threshold of Nurturance: A Fundamental Difference among Abusive Families" (Ryan, 1981) was circulated. This paper suggests a simple analogy that whereas families with physical abuse and neglect issues begin therapy "in the therapist's lap" (being nurtured and reparented) and become autonomous over time, families with incest issues begin at a distance, and lack of trust in the nurturer is a major challenge in treatment. Clients with physical and psychological abuse histories respond well to a safe "holding" environment that nurtures new growth, but a history of sexual abuse appears to jeopardize the participants' ability to tolerate or trust nurturance. Traditional counseling begins by establishing trust and then goes on to address the referring symptoms and issues, but a client whose trust has been betrayed by this most personal and intrusive

> In many cases the sexual aspect is less important in defining what is "different" in counseling regarding the sexual abuse issue than another aspect: the abuse of trust.

form of abuse may be unable to establish basic trust until much later in treatment. The challenge is to understand how to create a therapeutic relationship in the absence of trust.

Treatment of sexual abuse issues, regardless of the client's age or symptoms at the time of referral, must begin by creating a psychologically safe environment. The process of building therapeutic relationships parallels the parent-infant attachment process. Just as the infant is born into the care of the parent, arriving in that relationship with needs that require interaction to survive, the child or adolescent or adult who arrives in a therapy setting to receive care related to sexual abuse issues also needs care to support survival. Such survival ultimately must not be defined by abuse issues (an approach that perpetuates a victim stance) but rather by diminishing the risk of dysfunctional patterns of coping (which arise from a victim-victimizer model of attachment) by strengthening the positive growth and development of the individual. Such growth requires nurturance and interaction.

Imagining how to nurture a child victim comes easily, although the child's ability to receive nurturance may be quite limited. Older survivors may be effectively defended against nurturance, keeping a distance that is part of their strategy to avoid painful experiences. Nurturing those who have been abusive is most difficult, because the therapist is often as defended as the client.

The study group struggled to define and articulate the characteristics that underpin a successful attachment process, frequently returning to the concepts of "psychological safety" (Briggs, 1975; Ryan et al., 1988; Ryan & Blum, 1994) and "empathic care" (Steele, 1987a, 1987b, 1989). Briggs describes the following characteristics that support a sense of safety in relationships and enable nurturance to occur, even before trust is possible:

- Focused attention
- Nonjudgment
- Expressions of emotion
- Empathy
- Appreciation of diversity
- Trustworthiness

Steele's description of "empathic parenting" articulates the following process: the caregiver (1) reads the infant's cues, (2) forms a hypothesis regarding the meaning of the cue, and (3) validates the cue by meeting the need or expressing the emotion. This process validates the infant's own cues and its worthiness of care, as well as forming a basis for trust, trustworthiness, consistency, and communication. It is the infant's cue that stimulates the caregiver's response. Stern (1985) describes these responses as innate responses reflective of the caregiver's own experience of being an infant.

It was necessary to articulate the qualities of interaction that allow growth and development (and eventually the development of trust) in order to conceptualize a basis for interventions that could promote growth and foster trust. The analogy of the parent-infant interaction that enables the attachment process and the development of trust can be operationalized in interventions based on universal goals: communication, empathy, and accountability (Ryan et al., 1988, 1993; Ryan & Blum, 1994; Ryan, 1995).

The first goal, communication, is achieved by creating a language: words that can be used to describe life experience. Just as the parent-infant relationship begins with the struggle to communicate the infant's needs through an exchange of cues from the infant and interpretation by the parent (the baby cries and the parent must figure out what that cry means), the client presents the therapist with a series of cues that the therapist must interpret.

The second goal, empathy, is achieved by the therapist validating the client's experience — not by assuming that the client's perception is the same as the therapist's, but by facilitating the client's process of expressing the experience in his or her own way (Bennett, 1979).

The third goal, accountability, is achieved as the therapist encourages the "accurate attribution of responsibility" (Ryan & Blum, 1994; Ryan, 1995) by helping the client give up the blame and shame associated with the experience of helplessness, vulnerability, and incompetence and accurately attribute the responsibility for abusive behaviors to the perpetrator. In a parallel process, the client is invited first to become responsible (Jenkins, 1990) for his/her own behavior (especially choices related to any present symptomatic dysfunction) and second to reject responsibility for (and therefore the need to control) the behavior of others.

In processing victimization, it is necessary to recognize the perpetrator's responsibility while rejecting the role of victim as one's own identity. In a parallel process, sexually abusive clients need to accept responsibility for abusive behaviors, rejecting the identity of perpetrator as incongruent with their self-image. Every client must take responsibility for the ways in which he/she has been abusive to self and others. Although treatment begins by validating the abuse issues that are present in the contextual matrix, treatment must end by rejecting abuse as no longer definitive of the world, the self, and others.

For example, in the case of the young boy with abuse-related masturbatory fantasies, masturbation was clearly a high-risk behavior for this child, despite his use of appropriate privacy. The intervention in this case might be first to validate the reasonableness of the aggression-arousal connection in the context of his experience; then to help him articulate the confusion created when physical, emotional, and cognitive elements of an experience (i.e., sexual arousal, emotional fear, and cognitive confusion) are so incongruent; and then to help him avoid masturbatory behaviors when the abusive memories surface while creating nonabusive mental images to consciously pair with masturbatory behavior. Empowering him to be responsible for his fantasies increases his ability to accurately perceive his responsibility for subsequent behaviors.

Communication, empathy, and accountability become the tools the therapist relies on to facilitate the formation of a therapeutic alliance. Communication is the vehicle, and empathy is the goal. Accountability is the part of the intervention that accurately attributes responsibility in order to reject abuse and develop self-regulation (Ryan & Blum, 1994). The client (whether aged 4 or 40) must become responsible for his/her own way of expressing emotions in order to avoid abusive outcomes (Ryan, 1997). In treating perpetrators, the need for accountability is clear. We must recognize that it is equally important for victims to define the diverse ways in which they have become abusive to themselves or others or property and to take responsibility for avoiding perpetuation of destructive behaviors (Ryan, 1989).

Using the matrix as a guide, therapy pursues the following objectives:

- Establish a trustworthy and nurturing therapeutic alliance: a safe place for the client.

- Discover and articulate life history that describes the contextual matrix.

- Define abusive events.

- Express experiences in terms of emotion and become able to manage emotions.

- Understand the symbols and meanings the client has attached to the phenomena of abuse.

- Provide an opportunity to challenge those meanings and beliefs, and support cognitive restructuring to facilitate empathy and accountability.

- Correct distorted attributions of responsibility.

- Develop and internalize a mental representation of self as competent and trustworthy.

- Develop a mental representation of healthful relationships and attachment to others.

In the initial phase of treatment, while gathering information, taking histories, and making observations, the therapist is establishing the therapeutic relationship that will serve as the medium for growth and change. The therapeutic relationship models the establishment of attachment and trust in psychologically safe relationships. The healing nature of the relationship is present throughout the treatment process, even at the beginning of the initial assessment.

Assessment and intervention are concurrent and inseparable elements of the treatment, continuing throughout all phases as new information becomes available and the client experiences the validation of perceptual experience. Within this process, sound clinical assessments include the differential diagnosis of concurrent disorders that may be unrelated to the abuse issues yet influential in the matrix.

The intervention is based on a differential diagnosis that personalizes a treatment plan while encompassing diagnostic categories that have implications in treatment. For example, two people may experience very similar traumas and both show symptoms of PTSD, but management of their response and treatment planning may be very different when one also has a bipolar diagnosis and the other is experiencing a hypervigilant anxiety reaction or a dissociative response.

Some clients enter therapy for a presenting problem that seems to be unrelated to earlier sexualized trauma. For them, remembering events (and the associated affect) during the treatment process can disrupt current functioning as though those events had just happened. At such a time, the client may need containment and stabilization because the emergence of such content often comes with the full experience of thoughts, feelings, and behaviors that were never fully experienced at the time of the trauma. Dissociative responses that were employed to ensure the survival of the psyche at the time of trauma may give way in the presently safe and nurturing atmosphere of the relationship. This process allows the experience of the previously split-off or repressed impact to be realized in the present moment in a sort of time-released fashion. Thus the trauma is sometimes experienced by the client as if it were happening in the present, and he/she may need help in distinguishing between an earlier event and a current experience. In effect, the client needs a conscious awareness that it is now safe to experience what was too dangerous or overwhelming or incomprehensible to experience at the time of the trauma.

> The trauma is sometimes experienced by the client as if it were happening in the present, and he/she may need help in distinguishing between an earlier event and a current experience.

Especially when disclosure immediately precedes treatment, the client may need assistance in dealing with the immediate crisis and may need help to contain, manage, and stabilize the overwhelming emotions and chaotic cognitions of the here and now. Crisis intervention addressing immediate concerns in the client's current situation often requires the therapist to take on additional roles, acting as an advocate in placement, court, and/or Social Services decisions. For victims as well as abusers, the therapist must initially facilitate containment, stabilization, and organization for the client. This task may include helping the client become able to self-regulate and to develop an internal sense of control rather than manifesting the externalizing behaviors present in the client's dysfunctional cycles. In discovering the client's path through the matrix and his/her previous life experiences, the client benefits from validation of both past and present experience and from permission to express emotions and beliefs in his/her own way.

As the client becomes able to reveal (to himself/herself and to the therapist) the deep meanings he/she has attached to the phenomenon of abuse, the therapist supports the discovery and expression of these meanings by validating the client's unique response. The therapist considers not only what the client does and does not talk about but also *how* the client talks about it. There is as much information in the process of the therapy as in the content. The content describes the variables of the matrix, and the process describes the client's perceptual functioning.

Therapeutic Relationship: The Vehicle of Intervention

Sexual abuse occurs within the context of a relationship in an interaction between at least two people. If the quality of one's attachments colors all subsequent life experiences, it is imperative to understand the client's experience of self and other and how the client's internal models have been affected by the abuse. Therefore, it is within the context of another relationship, the therapeutic relationship, that understanding of these models occurs and can be challenged, supported, or altered.

The therapist invites the client to enter into a relationship so that together they can observe, understand, and mediate the effects of or adaptations to previous life experiences. As the therapeutic relationship develops and assessment and treatment evolve simultaneously, the unique and individual outcomes are identified as the client's own personal issues, characteristics, and manifestations. Interventions can then be directed by what has come from the client rather than relying on some preconceived menu of generic interventions.

The therapeutic relationship creates an opportunity for the client to revisit past experiences. The client reveals beliefs and behaviors regarding attachment through the description of those experiences.

The therapist invites the client to form an attachment in the therapeutic relationship and in so doing is able to directly observe the nature of the client's attachment pattern. Within the context of this therapeutic relationship, the client is offered an opportunity not only to work through the experience of abuse but also to reexperience the nature of attachment itself.

EXAMPLE 2:

Valerie sought therapy at the age of 43 for what she described as "family issues." She spoke of wanting to improve the relationships between herself and her husband and between her husband and their three children. She felt as though she and her husband could have been better parents, though she could not be specific about how they had erred. There was a sense of urgency in seeking help, as though time were running out. We noted that her oldest daughter was 18, a senior in high school, and that her emancipation from the family was imminent. The proximity of this transition made Valerie feel anxious and worried and provoked feelings of guilt.

Initially, therapy included marital sessions and several family sessions. Valerie's children were quite satisfied with the care they received from their parents and described favorable relationships with both parents. What they identified as difficulties in the family centered around their mother's preoccupation that she had not been a good enough mother. Valerie talked about her difficulty receiving positive feedback because of a persistent sense that she was somehow deeply undeserving and unworthy.

Valerie decided to continue in individual therapy and began the process of reexamining her own early history and relationships. What emerged was an image of a child lost in a family of nine children; being the next to the youngest, she felt overlooked. She described a classically avoidant attachment with her mother, citing examples of wanting to be physically close, but usually retreating when closeness was available. Valerie had spent many hours isolated and alone in a closet, soothing her sense of detachment by head banging and rocking while crying. She reexperienced feelings of sadness and loneliness as she recalled her sense of being different from the others and not belonging. As Valerie gained clarity and insight into these early conditions, she became overwhelmed by the feelings of loss and abandonment associated with her childhood perception of not being seen or understood. Her anxiety increased as she identified similar perceptions in her current life.

Because the focus in therapy was to address "relationship issues," the therapeutic relationship was under constant scrutiny. Many sessions were spent articulating Valerie's anxiety about depending on the therapist. As Valerie became aware of her dependence in the counseling relationship, she began avoidant behaviors, reflecting her fear that the therapist would abandon her. She expressed grief arising from her perception that the therapist would be unable to truly understand her or would be unwilling to take the time with her that she needed. She was sure that her needs would overwhelm the therapist, and she would alternate being angry with apologizing and wanting to take care of the therapist so that he wouldn't leave her. Valerie sought marital therapy with another therapist, interviewed other therapists for individual work, and frequently called anonymous crisis hot lines to help ease the tension of her dependence, as if she needed many caregivers to ensure that she would not be alone again.

Over time, the therapist provided consistent reassurance and a commitment to work with her until her work was finished. Drawing connections to her early attachments, it was possible to understand her expectation of a poor attachment in the therapeutic relationship. Eventually, Valerie worked through her anxiety and avoidant responses in the counseling relationship and began to settle into a healthy attachment that she could generalize into her relationships with her children and her husband.

Valerie spoke prophetically of the importance of the therapist being available to her, as if she sensed that she would need support for what was about to come up, though she was able to talk only vaguely about something ominous. She began to experience sensations she described as body memories: aching in her legs and feet and sharp pains or numbness in her hands. She talked more about a deep feeling of being bad or contaminated and a sense that she did not deserve to be alive. She made references to having the devil inside of her and described a longtime feeling of being evil. Memories of a time when she was 6 years old started to surface. What emerged was the recall of a series of ritualized sexual assaults by a dentist she saw several times in a short period of time.

Many months were spent remembering and interpreting the meaning of these bizarre and traumatic events. Based on her own perception, it was clear that the most traumatic element was the detachment she experienced from her mother, who never seemed to recognize that something terrible was happening to her at the dentist's office. She talked of the intense pain of not being seen or understood, and therefore not being protected. Rather than ask how the dentist could do the things he did to her, Valerie's question was, "How could my mother not see what was happening to me?" Because she had felt detached and alone and believed that she could count on only herself, she had relied on dissociative responses to cope with the overwhelming trauma.

Although Valerie continues in therapy at the time of this writing and the dissociation is the focus of her work, she talks about the healing nature of the therapeutic relationship, which has enabled her to feel safe and secure and trusting in current relationships. She talks about feeling more whole and integrated and has confidence that she is competent to complete her treatment successfully.

In Valerie's case, specialized interventions regarding sexual abuse and post-traumatic stress have been secondary to the treatment of the relationship disorder that was only circumstantially tied to her abuse issues. The dissociative defenses that protected Valerie as a child had become a hermetically sealed mystery, creating a sense of nonspecific anxiety and dread as a barrier to contentment and satisfaction in her current family.

Interventions Specific to Sexual Abuse

While we urge therapists to avoid adherence to a "recipe" for treatment, we acknowledge the usefulness of "measuring certain ingredients." Certain variables are present in all sexual abuse, and these can be explored to determine the extent of relevance. Each variable is present (more or less) whether the client is a recently victimized child, an adolescent or adult survivor, or a perpetrator of abuse.

To fully understand the client's experience of abuse, the therapist must consider the nature, duration, and frequency of the abuse. The nature of the abuse includes specific sexual behaviors, such as viewing pornographic materials, fondling, and oral or genital penetration. One must consider which behaviors were done to the victim, as well as which behaviors the victim was made to perform. Grooming behaviors include methods of engagement, such as the use of seduction, trickery, bribes, or coercion; threats of lost relationships, privileges, or attention; threats of force; or the actual use of force and violence. Duration takes into account the span of time and the client's developmental stages involved from the beginning to the end of the period of molestation. Frequency indicates whether the abuse was a one-time incident or repetitive or chronic.

The therapist must also consider the nature of the relationship between the abuser and victim in terms of roles and expectations:

identifying whether the two are strangers or well known to each other, of similar or different ages, or related to each other (e.g., siblings, cousins), or whether it is a primary caregiver relationship. The nature of the experience may be influenced by the dynamics of authority, dependence, trust, betrayal, coercion, and so on. The psyche has many different strategies for coping with experiences, depending on whether the interaction is perceived as an isolated incident or as an ongoing situation from which there appears to be no escape. Responses to abuse vary greatly and may result in functional defenses and coping or may result in post-traumatic stress symptoms or more severe dissociative responses, including dissociated identity disorder (DID; formerly called multiple personality disorder).

By posing gentle inquiries regarding the possible presence of these various characteristics, the therapist provides the language and the permission to speak about aspects of the experience the client has believed to be unspeakable. One step at a time, the therapist helps the client articulate his/her experience without being overwhelmed by the enormity of the whole memory. As the therapist observes client reactions to each piece, empathic recognition leads to validation of emotions and identification of salient issues. Throughout this process, the client may be revealing, through words or behaviors, the ways in which he/she has been accommodating and assimilating the abuse.

> **By posing gentle inquiries, the therapist provides the language and the permission to speak about aspects of the experience the client has believed "unspeakable."**

The therapist sets the stage for the interventions that will follow by making note of the client's strengths and expressing confidence in forecasts that follow each validation. For example, the query might be: "What did you think would happen if you did not comply when he told you to touch his penis?" ... "I see by your expression that you have some strong feelings about the threat of losing your family" (validation of the emotion associated with the threat) ... "You are becoming able to remember where that emotion began" (note of competence) ... "I am confident that you will become able to manage that feeling without being overwhelmed each time you feel threatened" (confidence in the future). The validation of the emotion is the primary intervention.

Later, the therapist might inquire about how the previously described aspect has been accommodated. For example, "I recall you telling me that you believed at the time that you would lose your family if you did not comply. What do you believe about that now?" In this query, the therapist focuses on the cognitions that have evolved. The intervention will be determined by the response, which the therapist may either validate or challenge. For example, if the client responds with a continued belief that he or she would have lost the family, the therapist may inquire if the client has evidence to support that belief. The therapist must not rush to reassure or confront the client's belief without going through the process of determining whether the belief is rational or irrational. Then it becomes apparent that the goal of intervention is to validate the belief using rational evidence, to challenge the distortion, or to provide new evidence that will make changing the belief rational by focusing attention on the evidence that contradicts it. As long as the client's current beliefs support a view that distorts responsibility (such as a child's responsibility to keep the family together), invalidates feelings (such as dismissing emotional cues), or suppresses communication (such as protecting dangerous secrets), the risk of abusive dysfunctions remains high (Ryan, 1989, 1995; Ryan & Lane, 1997).

As the matrix suggests, there can be enormous variations in psychological strategies for coping with and accommodating what may appear to be very similar events. There is no generalized and consistent one-to-one correlation between an event and a response. The therapist assists the client in describing experiences with words or play. The therapist and client together explore and discover the relevance of these variables, not as a basis for drawing assumptions about their meaning but as a means of describing the unique experience of the client. When the client's perceptions of variables are disproportionate to the content of what is described, the therapist may challenge the client to generate some hypotheses to explore the discrepancy, exploring whether the client is thinking in a functional or dysfunctional way. Specific and unique meanings of previous life experiences can predispose or shade the perceptions of each variable.

For example, an emotionally deprived adolescent girl (see "Cindy" below) perceived grooming behaviors, sexual innuendo, and seduction as indications of caring and attention. The therapist must determine whether such responses and meanings are distorted and need to be challenged, and what intervention will provide a rational solution. The therapist must begin by validating the experience and the client's interpretation as a reasonable defense before challenging the client to think differently. A survivor who internalizes responsibility and believes that he/she somehow caused the abuse may be likely to see other victims as responsible for their abuse. This interpretation may increase the survivor's chances of developing abusive behaviors and not recognizing his/her own responsibility.

Likewise, a perpetrator who believes that the child is responsible for "seducing" him/her remains at high risk to continue abusing. Such a client may have been made to feel responsible for the behaviors of others very early in life, may have arrived at that belief in a defensive strategy to feel more in control following uncontrollable experiences, or may have acquired the belief from cultural messages (such as common rape myths that blame victims). The distortion is best addressed at its point of origin and can then be followed across the life span to connect it to the rationalization of abusive behaviors. The therapist alternately identifies historical origins and challenges the client to see the parallels in recent functioning. For example: "What do you think the relationship might be between what your uncle told you and the abusive behavior that brought you into treatment?"

Another aspect of the sexual abuse that may require intervention is the nature of the disclosure. Some victims tell of abuse immediately, but many others delay disclosure for a variety of reasons, often in response to threats made by the abuser, or sometimes because of the person's own beliefs regarding the likely effects of telling. Some adults keep the secret of abuse for many years and make a disclosure while in therapy for other issues. When a disclosure is made, the therapist must pay attention to the client's perceptions of how people have responded to the disclosure in terms of being believed or not, of being protected or not. Sometimes the victim of sexual abuse is further traumatized by the response to the disclosure because he/she is not believed or is blamed and made to feel responsible for the event or for the effect of the disclosure separating the family. It is imperative for the client to understand how subsequent life experience either challenges or supports those perceptions and the meanings attached to them.

For both victims and perpetrators, interventions relevant to both the sexual and the abusive dynamics must be considered (Ryan, 1997;

Ryan & Lane, 1997). Exploration and assessment of memories, fantasies, and beliefs about sexuality (and their associated effects on current sexual arousal and behavior) are equally important for victims and perpetrators. Whereas arousal patterns have been a focus in offense-specific treatment of abusers, they are often overlooked in victim treatment. The effect of abuse on subsequent sexual functioning is always relevant. Similarly, the abusive aspects of the experience must be explored in order to assess the risk of abusive behaviors. Victims must be held accountable for abuse of self, substances, and/or property; all clients must take responsibility for perpetuating abusive interactions with others (Ryan & Lane, 1997).

Interventions Relevant to Age and Developmental Stage

To tailor interventions for the specific needs of each client, the therapist looks at the age and developmental stage of the client at the time of the abuse and at the time the client enters therapy. Even when the nature of the abuse is similar in a number of cases, the experience and meanings of the abuse can be interpreted very differently by clients at different ages. The client and therapist must also consider the previous life experience and identify and employ the skills and strengths that the client has already developed.

EXAMPLE 3:
Nicholas was 4 years old when he was molested by the adolescent son of his daycare provider. He disclosed to his mother after the third incident, despite the demands of the offender that he keep their "little secret." Nicholas was in an intact family with positive and secure parental attachments. He perceived the abuse as a very different kind of experience in his world, one that was uncomfortable, confusing, and threatening. When he turned to his parents for help, it was available: they believed him and took action immediately to protect him from further harm. He interpreted the experience as out of the ordinary and began to understand that although the world can be dangerous, he was not alone, and the family was a safe place where his needs would be met. The therapy supported his perceptions and reinforced his attachment to his parents while assigning responsibility for the abuse to the offender.

In contrast to the issues for Nicholas, consider the dynamics in the next example.

EXAMPLE 4:

Cindy, age 15, was raised in emotional deprivation and with poor early attachments. She was in and out of foster care from infancy and experienced gross inconsistencies in her caregivers. She longed for attention and nurturing and "just wanted to belong somewhere." When it seemed that her stepfather showed some interest in her, she was delighted. As he groomed her to accept his sexual advances, Cindy began to believe that the sexualized encounters were her opportunity to experience a sense of acknowledgment, importance, and belonging. Therefore she experienced some aspects of the abuse as nurturing and being cared for. She was reluctant to disclose the abuse, and she experienced loss when she was removed from the home and prevented from having contact with her stepfather.

Therapy for Cindy began by acknowledging her sense of loss and the legitimacy of her need to be taken care of. Only after those issues were identified and understood was she able to realize the inappropriateness of her stepfather's response to those needs and understand the selfish nature of his actions. Feelings of loss gave way to feelings of betrayal and anger as Cindy began to understand what appropriate nurturing looks like and experienced unselfish caring by her therapist. The actual treatment for the sexual abuse was secondary to the treatment for distorted attachments to abusive objects.

> **The therapist cannot assume that the adult's abusive behavior is necessarily a reflection of sexual deviance more than developmental or attachment issues, or that the adolescent is less of a risk to reoffend simply due to age.**

Similarly, those who provide treatment for the adolescent who abused Nicholas and the adult who abused Cindy must consider the differences relevant to age and developmental aspects. The therapist cannot assume that the adult's abusive behavior is necessarily a reflection of sexual deviance rather than developmental or attachment issues, or that the adolescent is less of a risk to reoffend simply due to age.

Child

The therapist gains insight into meanings by exploring the developmental tasks of the client at the time of the abuse. For a young child, abuse may interfere with or arrest development relevant to separation and individuation. This may affect internalization and identity formation. If abuse occurred during a preverbal stage, the disclosure and working through may be largely accomplished through the use of symbols and metaphor; treatment may best be achieved through play or other activities (such as art, visual imaging, or hypnosis) that rely less on verbal skills. Obviously, young children have the least amount of life experience to enter into the equation of understanding. Because of their age-related dependence and lack of socially sanctioned survival skills, there is often great pressure for young victims to accommodate to the abuse and to the environment in which it takes place. Adjusting to the situation is often their only choice, as they do not have the capacity to manipulate their external world. Other children may be "acting out" in attempts to reject the experience and take control externally. The child's helplessness, combined with the demands of case management, often requires that the therapist take on the role of child advocate within the family, Social Services, the justice system, and the community at large. When a child is acting out abusively, the therapist's role may also include advocacy for the protection of others.

Adolescent

When an adolescent presents for treatment of abuse that occurred earlier in childhood, more complex influences may be brought to bear by the increased volume of life experience. There may be delayed disclosure, with a concomitant negative influence on the adolescent's self-image and identity. Peer interaction in adolescence is crucial to creating a sense of belonging in the world, yet sexual abuse can have an isolating effect as a young person develops an insidious sense of being contaminated, damaged, or just different from others. Conflict, confusion, and tension may increase around the developing sexuality of an adolescent who was sexually abused as a child.

When an adolescent has been abused recently, the issues may be quite different. The adolescent victim's perception of sexuality and the meaning of sexual interactions is very different from the child's perception. With identity formation and self-image further developed, the adolescent victim may be even more likely than the child victim to believe that the abuse was deserved or provoked and to internalize responsibility for either attracting or failing to avoid the perpetrator's advances. The adolescent may also be more reticent to fully disclose due to a sense of privacy and beliefs regarding self-efficacy and protection. The peer group's facilitation or resistance regarding such disclosures and the initial reactions of peers may shape the path of subsequent life experience by influencing the victim's accommodation or rejection of the experience.

When an adolescent is referred due to his/her own abusive behavior, the therapist is again in a dual role of advocating for both corrective interventions and protection of others. As the therapy draws out the parallels between life experience and subsequent functioning, empathy and accurate attributions facilitate the process.

Adult

An adult brings the most complex life experience and may have a history of greatly delayed disclosure. Memories that have not been conscious for years may surface in the course of therapy for other issues. There may be a greater degree of cognitive distortion and deeply ingrained dysfunctional patterns, as well as the establishment of a sexually abusive cycle that is harmful to self or others. Although a recent study published by the federal government found the correlation between childhood sexual abuse and adult sexual offending inconclusive, there appears to be a correlation between a broad range of childhood maltreatment and the manifestation of abusive behaviors (Widom & Williams, 1996).

Adults are more likely to seek therapy due to some dysfunction that is causing them distress in current situations or relationships. Sometimes the abuse issues are identified as the referring problem, but often the client is not aware of a relationship between current distress and past experience. Helping the adult to make those connections as an explanatory bridge can dissipate resistance and minimization that might otherwise interfere in the treatment process. As suggested in Chapter 1, many of the dysfunctional outcomes for survivors develop as defensive strategies to manage overwhelming affect and cognitive confusion following events in childhood.

Whether the adult arrives in therapy with or without abusive dysfunctions as a referral point, the therapist must explore the client's behavior over time and be prepared to manage the implications of discoveries in terms of reporting both past victimization as a child and subsequent abuse of others.

Treatment Modalities

There are many different theoretical models and varying styles of intervention. Some interventions may be more useful in dealing with immediate crises in order to manage and stabilize current functioning. Other styles of therapy may intervene at deeper and more complex levels and include working through past experiences emotionally and cognitively to achieve integration. Whatever the therapist's theoretical orientation, if the client is viewed through the matrix, intervention and treatment will always be client centered and model the goals of communication, empathy, and accountability in order to reduce the risk of dysfunctional or abusive sequelae.

Based on the myriad variables in experience that may be relevant to the abuse issue, it is the responsibility of the therapist to develop differential diagnoses and treatment interventions for each individual client. The intervention may use one modality exclusively or move the client progressively from one to another. For example, intervention may begin in individual therapy and eventually move the client into group therapy, or the therapist may employ more than one modality at the same time. While individual therapy may be important in establishing a therapeutic alliance and assessing and interpreting the unique meanings of experience, some clients may be so distrustful of private one-on-one encounters that group work initially feels safer for them. Parent-child dyads or couples therapy may be useful when the results of the abuse (or of the treatment) affect dynamics in the client's significant relationships.

Family therapy is usually indicated when the client is young and is living in (or will return to) the home. Group therapy can be very useful at any age for its normalizing effect and the support of peers. Group work with families or peers has been favored as a norm for several legitimate and diverse reasons, including issues of cost, secrecy, and trust.

Cost

With limited funds available to treat victims and perpetrators, the cost-effectiveness of treating multiple clients in groups has been a way of attempting to provide affordable services.

Secrecy

Secrecy is a common denominator in sexual abuse for both victims and perpetrators. It is the element that allows abuse to occur undetected and discourages reporting. Often victims, perpetrators, and family members share the belief that something bad will happen if the secret is told. Symptomatic of the secrecy, victims and perpetrators of abuse often believe that no one else has experienced or can understand what they are going through. Group work provides a powerful experience of validation and reduces shame and stigma as it becomes apparent that the secret can be told and others can understand the issues.

Trust

Distrust of persons in a position of power or authority is a logical issue for victims (who fear being controlled or exploited) and is often a significant issue for perpetrators as well. Many victims cannot initially tolerate the intimacy of individual therapy and benefit from the security of numbers in a group. Both victims and perpetrators may initially resist group work due to the secrecy and stigma issues but express relief and are able to benefit from the support of a group once they get started.

For some clients, new attachments to group members provide renewed validation for the skills and trust that were betrayed in abusive interactions. For others, the struggle to create an attachment relationship in therapy is remedial, an entirely new experience of relationship and interaction. For the client who has never achieved attachment and trust, this new experience can mediate the negative effects of prior hurtful experiences and create the opportunity to redefine beliefs about self, other, and the nature of relating. An alternative model of relationships is possible, the internal working model is challenged, and a healthier view of nonabusive lifestyles becomes possible and rational.

> The "therapeutic relationship" is not always with the therapist. Sometimes initial sessions reveal that a child already has a secure attachment.

The "therapeutic relationship" is not always with the therapist. Sometimes initial sessions reveal that a child already has a secure attachment to a parent who is supportive and available. In such instances, the therapist's role may be to facilitate conversations between parent and child, that is, to be a resource to the parent. In family therapies, the goal is often to improve attachment and bonding within the family. Group therapies with peers who have similar issues may facilitate development of a primary attachment with a peer or even multiple attachments. Within a treatment milieu, many different experiences of relationship become possible.

By the end of treatment, the therapist and the therapeutic experience have become an integral part of the client's matrix, and the client's subsequent growth, development, and perceptions are changed by the intervention. The attachment formed in the therapeutic relationship allows the client to separate and move on, but it also constitutes a secure base to which the client can return in times of stress, when new developments in the ever-evolving matrix challenge the client's ability to continue integrating subsequent life experiences.

Much has been written regarding treatment techniques, exercises, and interventions for sexual abuse issues. Many are relevant and useful when applied differentially in the context of a therapeutic environment. It is the application of techniques on the basis of preconceived beliefs about referral client descriptors that reobjectifies clients in a process that parallels the depersonalization of abuse. No recipe can succeed without knowing "what's cooking" — how much of each ingredient went into the casserole. The thoughtful exploration of the client's matrix provides the basis for personalized interventions that are developmentally and contextually relevant to the individual.

The process of discovery constitutes an important intervention in and of itself, but it must be stressed that it does not stand alone. Treatment cannot end in validation and insight; remedial and corrective interventions are also necessary to moderate risks and develop optimal functioning. The discovery process provides the foundation for treatment planning and the rationale for focused interventions. A good treatment plan articulates specific goals and objectives. These objectives and the interventions to support success in reaching specific goals are described in the rich literature regarding psychotherapy in general and the treatment of sexual abuse in particular. The thoughts in this text do not replicate either general or specialized interventions but may support more comprehensive and holistic treatment plans.

The Therapist's Experience in Sexual Abuse Treatment

Courtney Pullen

We ask our clients to embark on perhaps the most coura-geous journey of their lives, and it is with the utmost respect that we initiate this arduous and rewarding journey with them.

Historically, professional psychological literature has only rarely discussed what impact prolonged exposure to abuse issues has on therapists and how such effects influence their ability to provide treatment. Exceptions to this observation include the extensive litera-ture on countertransference and, more recently, on professional burnout. However, neither of these topics adequately addresses the particular ways therapists are affected or the extent of the impact they experience as a result of working in the field of trauma.

In addition to the perils of professional burnout and the risk of countertransference, therapists working with abuse clients are per-sonally susceptible to experiencing secondary trauma, sometimes referred to as vicarious trauma. The concept of secondary trauma refers to emotional and psychological effects experienced through vicarious exposure to the details of the traumatic experiences of oth-ers. Vicarious trauma is described by McCann and Pearlman (1990) as the disruptive psychological effects often experienced by profes-sionals working with child abuse victims. They assert that, by being exposed to stories of abuse, the listener may vicariously experience abuse. These experiences are often emotionally painful and may have a traumatic effect on the listener. Similarly, chronic exposure to the distress of others may have a cumulative effect on the therapist's ability to cope with stress.

In this chapter, the discussion of secondary trauma expands on McCann and Pearlman's notion of vicarious trauma to include not only the experience of the victim's pain but also the therapist's exposure to the dynamics and deviance of abuse, including the perpetrator's mind-set and patterns of behavior and the victim's attempts to escape and cope with the abuse. Secondary trauma is described here as the disruptive psychological effects on those who work with abuse victims and/or perpetrators. Most therapists in the abuse field experience an impact on their personal lives, often feeling the same isolation and lack of support that is so pervasive in the lives of their clients. In addition, Chrestman (1994) found that therapists who work with trauma often experience a sense of intrusion and other problems related to behaviors associated with their clients' traumatic disclosures.

> **Most therapists in this field experience the impact of working with abuse issues on their personal lives.**

Most therapists have grown up in an environment of trust, believing in a society based on predictable rules, norms, and values. But exposure to the details of abuse tests therapists' basic beliefs about human nature. The journey through the client's memories of abuse is the most obvious component of the therapist's secondary trauma. Over time, daily exposure to worldviews and behaviors that are so different from the therapist's own and so intrinsically abhorrent causes changes in his/her own worldview. This vicarious learning requires the therapist to accommodate this new understanding of pain and abuse into his/her own view of the world.

Therapists who encourage clients to disclose the details of their abuse become increasingly vulnerable to the secondary trauma that can arise from listening to, and therefore experiencing, those disclosures. Recognizing the emotional challenges that face therapists and other "helpers" associated with abuse cases requires discussion of the therapeutic context. The circumstances that put professionals at emotional risk of secondary traumatization must be described before we can find ways to manage the effects of secondary trauma.

The Therapeutic Relationship

For the clients described throughout this book, abuse has occurred within the context of a broader relationship. Therefore, a vital part of the intervention must take place within the context of a therapeutic relationship. As described in previous chapters, the client's relational world is altered by abuse; he/she often has difficulty sustaining intimate relationships or relationships involving authority figures because abuse is rooted in the misuse of power. A therapeutic relationship involves both aspects: in the context of the therapeutic relationship, the therapist invites the client to reveal sensitive information and to accept the therapist as an authority who has information and expertise. Thus, the therapeutic relationship itself sets the stage for a perceived replication of interpersonal relations that the client's past experience suggests may be risky.

The therapist encourages the client to give up secrecy and any defenses the client has developed in order to feel safe. In an attempt to help the client integrate trauma, the therapist necessarily exposes the client to aspects of the abuse that he/she has defended against since its occurrence. Therefore, both the therapist and the client are vulnerable to secondary effects. The remembering and the hearing are both difficult. The process challenges the emotional limits and resources of both the client and the therapist. The paradox is that although the experience of participating as a listener in the traumatic events retold by clients is personally painful, the therapist's participation in the healing process with these clients is richly and personally rewarding.

The therapist must continually assess his or her own sense of self by looking for the optimal balance in the therapeutic encounter. The therapist provides a "container" so that the client can safely explore the vicissitudes of his/her feelings. The therapist must be fully present, but at the same time, the therapist's boundaries must remain fully intact.

Understanding the development of basic trust is essential in working with abuse clients. Many victims of abuse have had their worldviews completely shattered, leaving emotional scars, fragmented belief systems, and a lack of trust in themselves and in others. As a consequence of listening to the painful or traumatic stories of the clients, the therapist's sense of basic trust (and belief systems) also comes under attack. The need for safety is present in all therapeutic relationships, but it is particularly acute when working with abuse cases as a way to minimize both the client's and the therapist's stress (Erikson, 1959).

It is tempting to enter into the fray of the drama that unfolds in these situations. If therapists are not keenly aware of their own experience of the trauma story, they run the risk of allowing their own defenses to take center stage. Therapists may offer grand interpretations in an attempt to reassert authority or to distance themselves from the emotional pain of their clients' experience. Or therapists may find themselves being overfriendly in an attempt to avoid their clients' rage. It might be tempting for the therapist to believe the idealized transference. It might seem easy to give in to the client's "pull," to jump in and "fix it," yet it is imperative that the therapist simply hear and bear witness to the story and explore the impasse with the client, rather than try to eradicate the client's feelings.

Janoff-Bulman (1992) theorizes that survivors of trauma interpret subsequent information as consistent with their altered schemata. As the severity of the trauma increases, the worldview becomes dominated by it, and the survivor increasingly relates to others on the basis of the traumatic experience. This reenactment plays a vital role in the secondary trauma to the therapist, because the survivor engages others to take part in acting out the pattern. Herman (1992) writes that in this reenactment, the therapist (or any other person in the relationship) becomes a participant rather than an observer in the process. In essence, the therapist is induced to become part of the client's relational world and may fall into a variety of roles, depending on the form of abuse the client has experienced. For instance, in working with an incest victim, the therapist can experience the role of either exploiter or exploited. The reenactment of the abuse scenario sets the stage for struggles with the therapist's countertransference. In contrast, a therapist working with a perpetrator may feel either victimized or abusive. Either way, the therapist must guard against becoming part of the story, and in this internal struggle lies the experience of secondary trauma.

Manifestations of Secondary Trauma

In consulting with individuals and agencies that work with abuse cases, I have witnessed countertransference reactions pulling therapists in one of two different directions. The direction taken tends to be dictated by a combination of variables, including characteristics of the client; affective components of listening to traumatic stories; agency philosophies and expectations; and characteristics of the therapist, including his/her style of defending against emotional pain.

Some helpers defend against secondary trauma by emotionally distancing themselves, manifested in a variety of ways. Therapists may respond to pain by intellectualizing their assessment of their clients, by emphasizing only diagnostic impressions of clients, or by presenting sterile overviews of clients. The therapist's stance with the client may become detached and aloof in an attempt to remain separate from the emotional content of the client's story. When the therapist's own defenses are effective in isolating him/her from the client's pain, the therapist may minimize the abuse or feel contempt for the client's vulnerability and helplessness.

In this case, the therapist is emotionally removed from the room in an attempt to reestablish a personal sense of emotional safety. In this situation, it is likely that the client experiences the therapist's behavior in two ways: first, as abandonment; and second, as abuse (stemming from the disbelief and contempt the therapist is directing toward the client). In the therapeutic relationship, it is important to constantly be aware that abuse victims may be very attuned to other people's behaviors and moods, hypervigilant and hypersensitive to the cues that alert them to any perceived abusive pattern in others. Thus, they will be particularly observant of a therapist who is distancing and may perceive it as depersonalizing.

The other pull for therapists tends to be toward a blurring of the boundaries, becoming more of a caregiver than a therapist. The therapist's stance becomes that of the good mother who attempts to make up for past parental deficiencies. In this role, the therapist may overidentify with the client and, as a result, become unable to provide adequate mirroring and confrontation. It can also have the effect of infantilizing the client by giving the message that the client is fragile and unable to move forward without the therapist. This role generates dependency, and the therapist may start to feel overwhelmed.

> **The therapist may over-identify with the client, and as a result may become unable to provide adequate mirroring and confrontation.**

Further along the same continuum, the therapist may start to believe that he or she is the only person in the agency or community who really understands victims, creating an air of grandiosity on the part of the therapist. This dynamic, of course, creates a polarity in the psychological community as well as for the client. Unlike the prior example, in which the boundary between client and therapist is a rigid defense, in this situation the boundary is blurred. Both scenarios cheat the client: protecting therapists from their own fear and helplessness, and preventing them from being present with their clients.

It is the job of the therapist to create a safe environment where integration and resolution of painful and confusing experiences can occur. The client's pain and struggle must be met with sustained empathy. Yet, as the treatment proceeds, the client will begin to project trauma-specific transference that will have the potential to elicit complicated countertransference reactions and cause empathic strain (Wilson & Lindy, 1994).

Preparing Psychotherapists for Secondary Traumatization

Professional training prepares a therapist for a certain degree of dealing with others' pain and the impact of that pain by teaching about the concept of countertransference. However, what traditional psychology and counseling programs do not prepare students for is the experience of listening to the client's pain and the direct impact that these stories have on the therapist.

In classic psychoanalytic theory, countertransference refers to unanalyzed portions of the therapist's personality that either transparently or unwittingly interfere with the client's treatment (Epstein & Feiner, 1979). More recent conceptualizations identify two types of countertransference, positive and negative (Tauber, 1979). Negative countertransference refers to a situation in which the therapist intrudes on the therapeutic process because of his or her own unresolved issues. Positive countertransference refers to the utility of using the therapist's experience of the client in identifying the various parts of the client's inner world. In addition, the therapist can enter more fully into the therapeutic process by using his/her experience of the client to delineate the different aspects of the client's object world. Thus, positive countertransference can enliven the therapy by drawing attention to various themes or impasses that may be occurring in the treatment and that often parallel the client's experience in creating relationships outside of treatment.

While being aware of the potential pitfalls and values of using countertransference in the therapeutic relationship, the therapist must also be wary of the direct impact of secondary traumatization and, in particular, be able to recognize which of the therapist's schemata are challenged. Following is a sample of the primary areas that are frequently negatively affected through secondary traumatization.

Trust

A therapist working with abuse clients may hear dozens to hundreds of stories of atrocities that are beyond comprehension, in which a child's trust and entire sense of being have repeatedly been violated. These stories all involve the betrayal of trust by those who cared for the child, revealing the victim's perception of betrayal by those who failed to protect, as well as by the abuser. This takes a toll on the basic trust of the listener. The therapist may wonder whether any daycare center or neighbor is safe and start seeing or anticipating abuse around every corner. Fundamentally, it is difficult to trust in a world that can be so unsafe. This distrust creates fear that gets generalized to the therapist's most basic encounters. How many of us have experienced that awful feeling when our child walks out of sight around a corner in a store? As our hearts beat fast in the few moments it takes to locate the child, we have created nightmares of terrible possibilities.

Cultural Denial

Cultural denial about abuse serves many functions, primarily protecting people from an awareness of the extent of abuse in our society and how painful it is. For many people, this cultural denial is alive and well; however, those who work with either abuse victims or perpetrators are not afforded that luxury. The therapist's denial system comes under attack daily, listening to the horrible stories of intentionally inflicted pain and suffering. It is imperative that the therapist shed cultural denial as a protective device in order to truly engage with the client in his/her story, yet doing so creates vulnerability.

Vulnerability

We would like to think that we live in a world where we are safe and that we all follow certain moral laws of right and wrong. Yet the world of a therapist who works with abuse issues is filled with images of suffering and harm perpetrated on innocent people. It is hard to find a place in our minds for stories of child rape and physical abuse. It is difficult to hear about the neglect and disregard that leaves children and adults feeling that the abuse must have been, somehow, their fault. Listening to the pain described by innocent children touches our sense of vulnerability and powerlessness. Therapists may be moved to rescue both the clients and themselves from the pain. Therapists' inability to make sense of the trauma they hear parallels the clients' inability to do the same.

Splitting and Projection

With childhood abuse, it is common to witness the emergence of primitive human defenses, such as splitting and projection. As described in Chapter 2, it is common for children abused by a primary caregiver to preserve the relationship by separating or splitting the reality of the abuse from the caregiver, taking on responsibility for the abuse by perceiving themselves as bad and deserving of the abuse. In essence, it is easier for children to fathom that they are bad than it is to believe that, without cause, Mom or Dad did something bad to them. In this way, the child keeps the attachment to the parental object intact, and as a result, the child feels safer.

Particularly when working with abusive families directly or indirectly, the system outside the family may be the object of such primitive defense mechanisms. The caseworker or therapist who is intervening with the family often becomes the focus of projection and thus may be made the "bad person" who has "destroyed" the family. Some of these families are so good at this defense that an entire system of therapist, caseworker, lawyer, and so on may be in conflict, accusing one another of not doing their jobs. Thus, the system ends up demonstrating and reenacting the conflict of the family.

For example, a 13-year-old boy was placed in foster care as a result of his mother's abuse of him. For the first few weeks in the foster home, the boy expressed rage toward his mother and relief toward his living situation. In an attempt to be supportive, his foster parents teamed up against the "bad mother" by expressing their own rage at her abusive behavior. Within three weeks, the boy began to experience the loss of his mother and downplayed her long history of abuse. At the same time, he turned his rage toward his foster parents because they had been "saying bad things" about his mother. Understandably, the foster parents were dumbstruck. Their mistake was in over-identifying with one part of the boy while not taking the time to understand the totality of his feelings.

Isolation

The transfer of conflict and rage from the perpetrator to the therapist is often exacerbated by colleagues who do not understand childhood abuse or secondary trauma. This lack of sensitivity isolates the person who is working with victims of abuse, thus contributing to the secondary trauma experienced by the therapist. This dynamic can also occur in agencies where therapists who work with victims or offenders are left to manage their "troubled" caseloads on their own, without the support of colleagues, which is crucial to those who do this work.

> The therapist's experience can begin to mirror that of the clients: both therapist and victim/client are being "asked" by the perpetrator to be silent.

Secrecy

Secrecy and silence are the perpetrator's first line of defense. If secrecy fails, the perpetrator typically attacks the credibility of the victim (Herman, 1992). The therapist's experience can begin to mirror that of the client, in that both therapist and victim-client are being "asked" by the perpetrator to be silent. The client's need to talk about the abuse is frequently resisted by family members and friends who don't really want to hear about it. The message to the victim is, "I need you to be quiet about the abuse because hearing about it makes me uncomfortable." It is common for therapists to encounter a similar reaction from friends and colleagues. Thus, therapist and client receive the same induction: maintain the secrecy of the abuse.

A THERAPIST'S EXAMPLE:

What brought the impact of listening to traumatic stories to the forefront was finding myself involved in the same Wednesday night ritual for several months in a row. Wednesday was the evening I facilitated a group for men who had been sexually abused as children. I was able to cope with the horrible stories and tragedy by remaining distant yet supportive and caring, or so I hoped. Then I would delay going home until my wife would be asleep. Relieved to find her asleep (and able to avoid any physical contact), I would go to the basement, fix a strong drink, and stare at the TV, hoping to find that numb place where nothing really mattered. As I sat there with my drink, I would try to forget about the story of the man who had grown up with an alcoholic father and a psychotic mother. He spent most of his adult life trying to look normal in an attempt to escape the suffering of his childhood. He got married, quit drinking, fathered a child, and maintained a good job. Yet when he was not busy, he returned to his childhood and remembered his dad raping him and forcing him to have sex with his brother when he was 7. He came into therapy in an attempt to rid himself of this memory but found instead that he started to recall more of the abuse that he had experienced at the hands of both his parents. He described the sexual abuse in graphic detail, with scenes of his father forcing him to perform fellatio on an ongoing basis until he was a teenager.

Yet in all the litany of rapes, forced sex with an older brother, abandonment, and gross neglect, one scene still comes to my mind 10 years later. In this scene, my client described the deep longing he had for any kind of contact with his mother. She seldom held him or even touched him. However, on occasion, his mother would squat and urinate on him. He recalled that even though this caused him deep shame and revulsion, for that brief moment, it also felt good to have his mother close, to feel her warmth touch him.

As his therapist, I was left grappling with the images of him as a boy and the dreadful pain he had experienced. At the same time, I was struggling with how to be with myself and manage the overwhelming pain of these stories. I needed to leave the "safety" of my basement and reach out for support so that I could be available not only for my client but also for myself.

This oscillation was exacerbated by the understandable struggle this client had with trust. He continually vacillated between wanting to trust and disbelieving any offer of support that therapy would extend. In one session he would say that the treatment was too close and that he didn't trust the support and understanding. In another, the same overtures were described as aloof and distant. His favorite line was "get away a little closer." Besides being difficult for the client, this type of emotional oscillation gave me the experience of never quite knowing where the therapeutic relationship was and what was needed. My best attempts at interpreting this behavior as a repetition or transference did not make it any easier to remain present without personalizing the behavior. It was at times extremely difficult to maintain the necessary therapeutic neutrality.

Mediating Factors of Secondary Trauma

Understanding the effect of secondary trauma can minimize its impact on the therapist. However, this requires an understanding of its components. First are the qualitative components, the sheer impact of listening to the pain, deviance, and/or terror expressed by clients. As Judith Herman (1992, p. 140) observes, "Trauma is contagious." Just hearing the client's trauma story is traumatic. Second are the severity and length of the therapist's exposure to the trauma. To a degree, the longer and more severe the exposure, the greater the likelihood the therapist will experience the symptoms of PTSD. Last are the contextual components, the experiences and vulnerabilities the therapist brings from his or her own history. McCann and Pearlman (1990) view the therapist's unique responses to client material as shaped by both the characteristics of the situation and the therapist's unique psychological needs and cognitive schemata. They write that all therapists working with trauma survivors will experience lasting alterations in their cognitive schemata, which will have a significant impact on the therapist's feelings, relationships, and life.

Mediating factors need to be considered as well, such as the professional belief system of the therapist and his/her tolerance for ambiguity. Working with abused or abusive children or adults challenges the therapist's belief system and self-image personally and professionally. When stressed, it is human nature to become more rigid in our view of the world, yet the therapist needs to respond with flexible beliefs. In an effort to preserve the therapist's own view of the world, the realities of the client's world may be minimized or denied.

For example, a therapist may experience sexual arousal while hearing an account of sexual abuse, or the memory of a client's description of sexual abuse behavior may intrude into his/her thoughts while engaging in sexual foreplay with a partner. For a therapist working in isolation and operating with rigid beliefs about sexual abuse, such incidents might trigger distress or denial and put the therapist at risk of believing himself/herself incompetent, burned out, perverted, or worse. The dissonance created by the conflict among cognitive processes, emotional reactions, and physiological sensations is a typical reaction described by victims of sexual abuse. Yet the therapist may either deny the experience of this conflict or reach a distorted conclusion. A therapist with flexible beliefs and a collegial support system will discover that these experiences are related to vicarious exposure to secondary trauma and that they are normal. Specifically, such support systems can convey that (1) many therapists experience similar reactions; (2) the conflict parallels the victim's experience of the abuse; (3) these symptoms are manageable for the therapist (just as they are for clients); and (4) secrecy, isolation, and denial of these experiences by the therapist are nonproductive responses.

Denial isolates the therapist from the support that could facilitate resolution of these experiences and puts the therapist at risk in daily functioning. Isolation is an important symptom of secondary trauma and can exacerbate the trauma itself. The therapist's understanding of his/her own secondary experience can illuminate what the client is struggling to understand and, in that way, can be beneficial to the treatment at hand — but only when the secondary trauma is understood and under control.

A sense of personal safety comes from believing in a world that has clearly established rules and norms. But working in the abuse field exposes therapists to a great deal of ambiguity and uncertainty, not to mention a world that is not benevolent. Acknowledging the risks associated with this work sets the stage for prevention. The following suggestions for self-care can aid therapists in using a proactive, preventive strategy.

Internal Self-Care

1. *Expect countertransference reactions; it's a normal part of treatment.* Use positive countertransference to inform yourself about what is being played out in therapy. Use negative countertransference to inform yourself about what is happening internally.

2. *In session, stay separate.* Maintain your awareness of what is going on, and don't forget to breathe. While conducting a seminar for a group of colleagues, Carl Rogers realized that one of the most important self-care techniques he used as a therapist was to silently remind himself that he is OK. Remember that you too are OK, and your "OK-ness" remains intact even when listening to the horror of abuse.

> **Your own therapy may help get you through the effects of secondary trauma.**

External Self-Care

1. *Arrange for supervision with a therapist experienced in trauma work.* This step will reduce your isolation and provide you with the personal and professional support that is critical to professionals engaging in this work.

2. *Connect with other professionals in the field.* One of the great values of our study group is the ability to ask for and receive feedback and support. The study group provides both personal and professional support and is useful for those times when we cannot see the difference.

3. *Allow yourself your own therapy.* In this way, you are relinquishing the need to carry the load by yourself. Your own therapy may help get you through the effects of secondary trauma and allow you to understand those personal parts that contribute to your countertransference with clients.

4. *Allow yourself to have a personal life.* Balance your professional and personal lives. Seek the support of friends and family.

5. *Seek balance in your professional life.* Arrange time in your day for breaks, and limit the number of sessions you conduct, particularly with trauma clients. Whenever possible, work with a mixed caseload.

6. *Be aware of your personal signs of burnout.* Often, one of the first signs of burnout is that we forget what has worked to alleviate the effects of burnout in the past, so we keep repeating past mistakes. Here are some things that help us avoid burnout:
   - Take walks inside or outside and give your mind and body a break.
   - Play with your children, or someone else's children; there is no better way to give your mind a rest.
   - Exercise in whatever way suits you.
   - Get a massage — you deserve it.
   - Take vacations regularly on a beach, in the mountains, on a river, but not at a conference.
   - Read for fun (when is the last time you found a journal article fun?).
   - Tune into the comedy channel — laughter can indeed be the best medicine.
   - Watch fun movies — again, the laughter thing.
   - Be silly — you're never too old.
   - Throw darts, play pool, and go bowling all in one night.
   - Meditate — take time for quiet.
   - Hike — take time to smell the flowers.
   - Ski on water or snow, and go as fast or slow as you like.
   - Go fishing even if you throw the fish back (or don't catch any); the serenity is worth it.
   - Partake in art and music — explore your creative side.
   - Pursue a hobby, and if you don't have one, get one.

As professionals beginning to understand the devastation of psychological trauma, we are constantly reminded of our own vulnerability, and the temptation to ignore or discount victims is great. Historically, the psychological treatment community has pathologized victims and, at times, has normalized or excused the perpetrator's pathology. As society has begun to listen to victims and take them seriously, their numbers have grown under the light of recognition.

As more children and adults have come forward to speak of the devastation of their abuse, the psychological and other professional communities have responded by creating laws, conducting research, refining therapeutic techniques, teaching, and taking political action. But many of these professionals burn out and leave the field. Denial of the fact that people are personally changed by this work significantly contributes to this attrition.

Inroads into curbing the horror of psychological trauma are being made as the result of a multidisciplinary approach. If progress is to continue, those who treat victims and perpetrators of abuse must themselves remain healthy. When the commitment, integrity, and willingness of the helpers are "burned up," this creates a professional "victim."

Secondary trauma is a process that all professionals who have worked with abuse victims have known and experienced. Listening to stories of trauma and becoming part of an abuse client's relational world change the helper. The results of secondary trauma may include some of the same symptoms and defensive strategies that victims and perpetrators bring to treatment, including personal and professional isolation and the risk of compensatory behaviors. Therapists benefit from the same advice as clients: reach out for support.

8

Recent Developments and Conclusions

Gail Ryan

Over the past decade, the body of literature on sexual abuse has grown obese. Whereas in the early 1980s it was possible to collect, review, and maintain a complete library on the subject, by 1990 the sheer number of volumes was out of control; today, it is virtually impossible to review all that is being written. It has become difficult even to afford to buy, much less read, the numerous specifically relevant journals, not to mention the difficulty in locating articles published in a wide range of discipline-specific journals. Books, monographs, reports, workbooks, and curricula abound; it has become difficult to separate substantive new information from reformulations of earlier work. At the same time, the number of conferences, workshops, and training opportunities has proliferated as well, a source of insight into the newest and most recent developments. The field is suffering from "information overload," yet so many questions remain unanswered.

In recent years, the study group has found some of the most intriguing information in the surrounding psychology, sociology, neurology, and developmental literatures. The contextual matrix and the dysfunctional response cycle, combined with developmental models (such as Strayhorn, 1988), have taken on additional importance in guiding our search for new reports and theories related to contextual, dynamic, or developmental variables that might be relevant to our initial question.

This chapter reviews some of the new ideas in the field that have resonated with our experience, brought new implications to bear, or increased our understanding or curiosity regarding the developmental-contextual approach. Some of these ideas fit snugly in place in relation to the matrix or the cycle previously described. Others stand alone, inviting in their relevance but not yet fully integrated in our thinking. It seems fitting to begin these concluding remarks by revisiting some of our earlier hypotheses.

Victim to Victimizer

In the early days of sexual abuse work, it was believed that although the vast majority of sexual abuse victims do *not* become sexually abusive to others, the vast majority of those who are sexually abusive had been sexually abused. Yet over the years, many samples of sexual abusers have reported a widely discrepant range of sexual victimization histories.

In data from 90 programs admitting sexually abusive youth, approximately 40 percent of the clients were known to have been sexually abused, and 40 percent had been physically abused (Ryan, Miyoshi, Metzner, Krugman, & Fryer, 1996). Although this finding is 2½ times the incidence of sexual abuse in the general population (Timnick, 1985, and Finkelhor, Hotaling, Lewis, and Smith, 1990, reported that a *Los Angeles Times* poll found 16 percent of American males reporting sexual victimization), it is still less than was initially believed. Several other studies have reported a similar incidence of sexual victimization, including Hunter's (1996) study of victim-to-victimizers. Yet it has become apparent that in most samples, with the inclusion of physical violence, sexual abuse, and parental neglect as "maltreatment" factors, almost the whole population has experienced some type of maltreatment (Hunter, 1996; Ryan et al., 1996). Recently, a monograph released by the U.S. General Accounting Office reviewed 22 retrospective studies of adult sex offenders, 1 study of sexually abusive adolescents, and 2 long-term prospective studies that followed two groups of children

> **Over the years many samples of sexual abusers have reported a widely discrepant range of sexual victimization histories.**

who had experienced abuse (Widom, 1992, 1996; Williams, 1995). That report concludes, "[T]the experience of childhood sexual victimization is quite likely neither a necessary nor a sufficient cause of adult sexual offending" (Widom & Williams, 1996, p. 5). That report expresses some surprise about findings in the prospective studies that suggest that children who had experienced physical abuse or neglect developed sexually abusive behavior even more often than those who had been sexually abused. These trends in research seem to support our hypotheses regarding the complexity of correlations between antecedents and outcomes.

In other developments arising from work with sexual abusers, Hunter's review of several studies measuring sexual arousal patterns of sexually abusive youths indicates that sexual deviance may be less of an issue with them than was originally believed. Male youths who were molested by males and exclusively molest younger male victims appear most likely to have deviant sexual interest and/or arousal as adolescents (Hunter, 1996; Hunter & Becker, 1994). He points out that much of the work with sexually abusive youths arose from models developed for adults and suggests that this issue needs to be revisited from a developmental perspective.

Influenced by this group's work, Ryan (1997) introduced a developmental-contextual approach for differential diagnosis and treatment of sexually abusive youths. This approach was described in the 1996 Safer Society Foundation Sexual Abuser Treatment Program Questionnaire as follows:

> A holistic approach based in theories of developmental competency and phenomenology. Primary emphasis on 1) Promoting growth and development as a means to correct deficits and/or deviance reflected in the cognitive-behavior pattern; and 2) Challenging "view of the world" through empathic recognition and validation of the differential needs and emotions of self and others.

Similarly, work with victims and survivors may benefit from appreciation of a developmental-contextual approach.

Concurrent Risk Factors

Even before the original "Victim to Victimizer" paper had reached publication (Ryan, 1989), another working group at the Kempe Center that was developing a curriculum regarding children's sexual behavior (Ryan et al., 1988) had hypothesized that the risk of children beginning to engage in sexually abusive behaviors involving other children might be increased by a variety of "nonsexual risk factors that seemed to be overrepresented in samples of sexually abusive adolescents, including parental loss, inconsistent caregiving, nonnormative environment, and some concurrent psychiatric disorders. These hypotheses arose from our own clinical experiences and were reinforced by findings from several studies in progress looking at developmental variables (Prentky et al., 1989; Gilgun, 1988; Law, 1987; Ryan et al., 1996). Each of these areas of risk has continued to attract interest, and numerous references have emerged in research and theory that expand support for thinking that the etiologies of the long-term outcome categories in the matrix are multifaceted and uniquely individual.

Attachment

Numerous groups are looking at how various aspects of attachment affect and are affected by internal working models when sexual abuse is present. Questions about attachment models have frequently appeared in the literature discussing the vulnerability and resiliency of child victims, and attachment "disorders" have been cited in relation to the development of sexually abusive behaviors in young children. However, despite the frequent mention of attachment models in relation to physically abusive or neglectful parents, only recently have researchers studying adult and adolescent sexual offenders begun to consider the attachment patterns of sexual perpetrators (Marshall, Hudson, & Hodkinson, 1993; Ward, Hudson, Marshall, & Siegert, 1995).

Marshall, Ward, and Hudson, in a series of papers and presentations with other colleagues, have demonstrated application of a model that explores relationships between attachment style, internal working models, interpersonal goals and strategies, intimacy deficits, loneliness, and sexuality. They have been able to draw distinctions relative to the modus operandi (specifically, characteristics of offending) of different subtypes of sexual offenders based on these factors that may have far-reaching implications in prevention, treatment, and relapse prevention. They have tentatively described differences in the cognitions and grooming processes of perpetrators on the basis of their attachment models (readers are urged to access and continue to follow this work).

Attachment disorders in young children have been discussed by many authors in relation to emotional and behavioral disturbances. This recognition has supported efforts to provide therapeutic interventions in the parent-child relationships of behaviorally disturbed children and has been an important area of work with sexually abusive children and adolescents as well. An interesting article by Lieberman (1996) discusses aggression and sexuality in relation to toddler attachment from a developmental perspective, which may further illuminate thinking about the onset and maintenance of sexual behavior problems.

Radke-Yarrow et al. (1995) studied the development of attachment in the context of high-risk conditions (such as maternal depression) and found support for consideration of development in interaction with other relationships and conditions. Their appreciation of the way conditions are expressed in the environment in combination with the child's style of coping is congruent with our thinking about vulnerability.

In much of the attachment work, it appears that theorists and researchers begin with an assumption that if the mother figure is present, that relationship is where the primary attachment will originate and, therefore, that relationship will form the basis of the child's internal working model. Since one of the constants in our course of study has been to question the validity of assumptions, it seems important that the exploration of attachment issues begin with the question, "Which relationships have been the primary attachments for the individual, and how consistent or disrupted have those relationships been?" Then the question regarding multiple attachment relationships would be, "Which relationship is reflected in the individual's internal working model?"

It is my belief that we often overlook or minimize primary attachments to siblings, paternal figures, or other early life relationships that in some instances may be more salient than the mother-child relationship in understanding the phenomenology of the client. A few examples from clinical practice illustrate the importance of sibling and extended family relationships.

> **We often overlook or minimize our attention to primary attachments to siblings, paternal figures, or other early life relationships which may be more salient than the mother-child relationship.**

EXAMPLE 1:

In one family, two sons had both been sodomized. The older boy, A, was victimized by a cousin who was the son of A's favorite aunt, on whom he had relied for positive attention throughout his life. The second son, B, was subsequently sodomized by A. It seemed apparent that A's primary attachment was to his maternal grandmother, with whom he had spent much of his early life. The role of the maternal aunt (who had been a young adult in the grandmother's home when A was small) was completely overlooked. It was also apparent that A had been severely physically abused by his biological father as an infant but had a strong bond with his stepfather, who was severely abusive to B. B was described as a difficult child and was abused by both parents prior to Social Services interventions. It seemed as if he was lacking in any primary attachments.

Both boys did poorly during the first year of treatment and were very resistant. Only during the second year did some of the critical information emerge.

A had initially claimed that his own sexual victimization was perpetrated by a teenaged baby-sitter because he feared that naming his cousin would result in his aunt abandoning him. When he finally revealed the secret regarding the true identity of the perpetrator, he became able to take responsibility for his own abusive behaviors, and treatment progressed rapidly. It then became apparent that A's sodomy of B was a culmination of lifelong physical and emotional abuse of B by A, beginning when A attempted to strangle the infant B in his crib. The parents had empowered A to administer violent disciplinary beatings for them after Social Services restricted the parents' violent behavior in the home. After A took responsibility for his own abusive behavior, B was able to disclose that he had also been abusive, molesting a younger sister and threatening her with guns and knives.

Treatment might have moved more quickly if all of the extended family and sibling relationships had been assessed for attachment earlier in the process. It is ironic that this family's entry into treatment was the referral of A as a sexual perpetrator. The focus on A's sexual offense was a critical element in his treatment, but it also became apparent over time that A was the healthiest person in the family and had the best prognosis because he had the asset of primary attachments to his grandmother and aunt outside the violent family, resources that had not been available to his siblings.

EXAMPLE 2:
Initially referred for sibling incest, a brother and sister were only one year apart in age, and both described the brother as the protector and nurturer in a violent, disorganized household. The mother was equally clear that the brother represented the sister's primary attachment figure, having fed and cared for her from birth while the mother and father were involved in domestic violence and alcoholism. Despite extensive incest-related treatment, the sister continued to do poorly, engaging in self-destructive and high-risk behaviors. Only when she was able to fully describe her relationship with her brother did it become apparent that he had also been pervasively physically abusive toward his sister throughout their lives. In spite of the violence in the sibling relationship, he was also her protector and extracted sexual favors from her by threatening to leave her alone at home.

As Roland Summitt writes: "Such trauma bonding which seems bizarre and paradoxical to outsiders occurs by being both the most vital and most abusive relationship in life. The victim becomes morbidly dependent and helpless even to conceptualize another way of life" (personal communication, 1997).

EXAMPLE 3:
The family history clearly described a primary attachment between a 12-year-old boy and his two older sisters who had been primary caregivers while their mom worked and went out to bars. At age 4, the boy was thought to have been sodomized by an uncle when he was sent away to be cared for by relatives. Subsequent problems with enuresis and encopresis resulted in shaming and intrusive caregiving by the boy's mother when he returned home. For this boy, the most potent treatment issues were initially thought to be (1) his mom's neglect in the early years, (2) trauma while placed with relatives, (3) his mom's poor response to his toileting problems, and (4) the boy's sexually abusive behavior toward his nieces and nephews, the referring problem.

Some thought was also given to the absent father issue, since the mother had not married and the boy had no knowledge of his father.

With such a full plate of diagnostic areas, treatment almost missed the significance of sibling loss for this boy. His placement with relatives was triggered by the sisters' becoming unable to care for him because of their own busy high school schedules. When he returned home, both sisters were away, involved in young adult relationships that produced children. The boy's sense of abandonment and displacement in his primary attachment to his sisters was never articulated or resolved. His abuse of the nieces and nephews was clearly a retaliatory behavior, driven by his need to betray his siblings as he perceived they had betrayed him.

Concurrent Psychiatric Disorders

Among the nonsexual risk factors associated with dysfunctional outcomes following sexual abuse, it has been suggested that some concurrent psychiatric disorders are especially relevant — in particular, anxiety and/or depression, obsessive-compulsive disorders, attention-deficit disorders, and post-traumatic stress disorder (PTSD). With any dual or multiple diagnosis, it is important to think about both the symptom interactions and the origin of the disorder. For example, PTSD may be present but cannot be assumed to be a product of sexual victimization. PTSD can result from earlier physical or psychological assaults or any traumatic life experience in which the client perceived a complete loss of control and a sense of helpless vulnerability (Terr, 1991).

In the previous example of the two brothers, brother A appeared to have had a PTSD reaction characterized as a flashback that was related to his single sexual assault of his brother. He described that assault as "weird, because I kept feeling like I was [my cousin] and like B was me ... I did the very same things ... I even said the same things that [my cousin] said to me." For A, physical abuse was congruent in the home and less traumatic than the sexual assault by his cousin, which occurred while he was visiting a safe and trusted extended family.

In contrast, in the brother and sister example, the boy did not describe any traumatic characteristics related to his own sexual victimization by a visiting relative or to his sexual abuse of his sister. Yet he was extremely sensitive to trigger issues for his abusive cycle, and he would become anxious and cognitively disorganized and would dissociate whenever he was pushed to examine these vulnerability issues. His dissociation seemed to be wired to his vulnerability for physical assaults due to the domestic violence in his home, including having been thrown through a window when his father was in a violent rage.

Both young perpetrators, brother A and the brother in the brother-sister example, demonstrated the maladaptive pattern represented in the cycle, but they needed different interventions in treatment. For brother A, treatment of the PTSD could be accomplished by a process following Spiegel's (1993) eight Cs of PTSD treatment (see Figure 8.1). For the brother in the brother-sister example, however, treatment could not begin to approach the relevant issues until

> **Both young perpetrators demonstrated the maladaptive pattern represented in the cycle, but they needed different interventions in treatment.**

neurochemical medications were used to decrease his anxiety and dissociation. With medications, the boy was able to tolerate the work of desensitizing the issues of vulnerability. By the end of treatment, medications were no longer needed.

The research on PTSD, especially that of van der Kolk and colleagues (1987), has been very useful in describing the neurological effects of trauma and their relationship to subsequent symptoms. If the delicate balance of serotonin and norepinephrine secretions in the brain is permanently altered by a traumatic experience, subsequent events reminiscent of some component of the trauma may trigger a state of hyperarousal that overwhelms normal coping strategies. Perry (1993) writes that the brain grows and develops in a use-dependent way, which requires new experiences to be retrained. When the individual experiences a hyperarousal response, the cortex of the brain cannot function in its usual fashion, and disorganized thinking and defensive responses are common symptoms.

Another cluster of symptoms that may benefit from neurochemical interventions is the presence of intrusive images and/or fantasies. These may be associated with premorbid obsessive-compulsive characteristics that rise to a clinical level following a trauma, or they

Figure 8.1   The Eight Cs of the PTSD Treatment Process

---

1. **Confrontation:** Careful history gathering to verbalize traumatic events.
2. **Condensation:** Gathering relevant pieces of memory that can be integrated into a memory representative of the traumatic time.
3. **Confession:** Dispelling guilt or shame associated with traumatic victimization in order to validate the helplessness or lack of control (which is guiltless).
4. **Consolation:** The therapist expressing feelings that validate (e.g., "Hearing about your experience makes me very sad … I am sorry this happened to you") and comfort or give encouragement and hope (e.g., "I believe you will be able to manage these memories").
5. **Consciousness:** Becoming able to remember is dependent on developing a belief that the client now has resources to face and manage that were not available at the time (acknowledgment of utility of previous defensive strategic acts to congratulate survivorship).
6. **Concentration:** Focusing work on remembering (or hypnosis) provides discrete blocks of time to manage the affect brought up with memories (e.g., "put on the shelf," "open the box," or "closing the book/journal").
7. **Control:** Working to achieve an internal sense of control, the ability to manage memories. Cognitive techniques may be taught regarding controlling one's thoughts.
8. **Congruence:** Overcoming the dissonance of the trauma so that it can be integrated into the concept of self as one part of a continually evolving identity. Restructuring thoughts about the trauma so that it is neither denied by nor definitive of the individual.

Source: Adapted from Spiegel, D. (1993). Eight C's of traumatic dissociation therapy. In *Dissociative disorders: A clinical review.* Lutherville, MD: Sidran Press.

may be the post-traumatic flashbacks of PTSD, which trigger compulsive, ritualized coping strategies. In either case, there is a high risk of hypersexuality, which may increase the risk of revictimization, promiscuity, or abusive sexual behavior.

Diagnoses that are often present in combination with negative sexual abuse sequelae include the behavioral disorders described in relation to the cycle as abusive to self, others, or property. The cycle represents compensatory or retaliatory reactions that may be exacerbated by premorbid conditions. For example, bipolar depression is thought to be a genetic predisposition, but it may not become apparent until the individual's coping mechanisms or neurological functioning is stressed. Sometimes symptoms of sudden, extreme mood swings, deep despair, volatile anger, and/or extreme irritability can be traced as occurring prior to the referring abuse issues, but even a situational depression with or without intermittent rages may require medical management to reduce the risks of suicidal despair or other dangerous defensive solutions. Alternatively, despair, sadness, and anger may be explicitly tied to the abuse incidents. Bipolar disorder may also be exacerbated by treatment interventions, and the client who has intense mood swings may resist the clinical work due to a fear of losing control. This is another instance when the most sensitive treatment issues may overwhelm normal functioning; successful treatment may depend on appropriate pharmacological management.

Anxiety disorders may have been at a subclinical level prior to treatment but escalate into panic or dread as the client fears reexperiencing traumas and shifts defenses during the treatment process. Although most clients do not need medication, some do; the client's willingness to endure the painful aspects of treatment can be increased by the use of appropriate medications. Clients who consistently resist painful issues because they fear that they will be overwhelmed or lose control may be right and should be referred for psychiatric evaluation of pharmacological intervention options.

In children, attention deficits can make it particularly difficult to maintain a focus in treatment, and hyperactivity may exacerbate behavioral symptoms. Attention-deficit hyperactivity disorder (ADHD) may be overrepresented in groups of sexually preoccupied victims, and they may be particularly at risk for sexual acting out for several reasons. The hyperactivity associated with attention deficits is thought to be related to imbalances in brain chemistry that occur when levels of certain chemicals dip too low without stimulation (Ross, 1996). Therefore, the child diagnosed with an attention deficit may be seeking optimal levels of stimulation by acting out in ways that create increased arousal (attention seeking, risk taking, sexual stimulation, substance use, and so on). Impulsivity may be characteristic as well, and may lead to acting without thinking.

The attention deficit may also interfere with the client's ability to attend to the social and interpersonal cues that should shape empathic relationships. Failure to recognize the distress cues of others may contribute to the client's risk of boundary violations and intrusive or abusive behaviors. In addition, social skills deficits and poor self-image, which are common by-products of ADHD (associated with negative interpersonal feedback), may position the ADHD child in a significantly younger peer group than the child's chronological age, providing access and opportunity to exploit these younger peers.

Finally, there is a tendency for persons with attention deficits to become preoccupied with pleasurable activities that provide high levels of physical and neurochemical reinforcements, and these behaviors become habituated over time (Ross, 1996). Clinicians are encouraged to remember that although the hyperactivity characteristic may become less apparent with age, attention deficits appear to be more stable over the life span and should be assessed in clients of all ages. The risks of arousal seeking and the client's inability to maintain focus are amenable to pharmacological treatments. At the same time, such symptoms must be distinguished from the client's inability to focus on specific issues that are causing discomfort; this discomfort avoidance can be resolved with psychotherapeutic interventions.

Phenomenology and Ecological Issues

Several other areas of study have emerged that are both congruent with and enhancing to the developmental-contextual approach to understanding sexual abuse issues. Just as the study group recognized the relevance of the unique matrices of family members and professionals with whom the client interacts, some ecological models view the sexual abuse incident as the central point in the concentric rings of a "ripple effect." Ecology lends itself to exploration of the influences and interactions of the multiple systems surrounding the individual: family, community, and society.

The individual does not exist in isolation, nor do victims and perpetrators experience sexual abuse without interacting with the rest of the world. Gilgun is one theorist who studied the isolation factor in relation to the processes of sexual exploitation (Gilgun & Connor, 1989) and has gone on to create an ecological model (Gilgun, 1996). An ecological perspective can be useful in the discovery process described in Chapter 5 because it encourages casting a wide net and sorting through each layer of influence in order to fully describe the client's view of the world.

There is little doubt that the beliefs and norms of the family and community may profoundly affect both victims and perpetrators by shaping their perceptions of abuse. In countries that outlaw corporal punishment, it is known that not all adults will refrain from either purposefully or impulsively striking children. What is expected, however, is that when children are hurt by caregivers, the child's perception will be that such behavior is due to the parent's failure to control impulses or to employ other management strategies rather than proof of the child's own badness. The goal is to shift the attribution of responsibility so that children do not internalize violent behavior and physical force into their own worldview and self-image.

Similarly, we can hope that ecological changes in attitudes regarding sexual abuse will create more accurate attributions of responsibility, so that families and communities assume greater responsibility for keeping children safe and potential perpetrators become less able to externalize responsibility for their behavior. Such shifts in the belief system of the child's environment, following the greater awareness working to dispel the secrecy, may make it easier for children to recover without internalizing any stigma. There is already some

> **We can hope that ecological changes in attitudes regarding sexual abuse may create more accurate attributions of responsibility.**

evidence that children find it easier to report abuse as a result of awareness education in the community.

Ecological perspectives have implications in all levels of prevention and intervention for both victims and perpetrators. Readers are encouraged to follow the development of these models in the literature. The ecological models surround the contextual model that describes the unique experience of the individual. Developmental models are at the heart of these concentric models (see Figure 8.2).

For purposes of treatment planning, our study group has paired the contextual matrix with Strayhorn's (1988) developmental description of the psychological health skills that constitute optimal human functioning (see Figure 8.3). Strayhorn's model describes 62 observable signs of these developmental skills.

We have been concerned that too much work related to sexual abuse has focused on the deviant experience and not enough on healthy growth and development. The concept of pairing development

Figure 8.2   Ecological Model

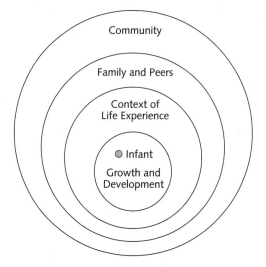

and experience is apparent in Gilgun's (1996) model of risks and assets, wherein she supports differential diagnosis and treatment by assessing both positive and negative factors. Treatment goals are designed to moderate the effects of risk factors and enhance the weight of assets. The risk factors and the assets may be internal, external, and/or ecological in nature. By distinguishing case characteristics in this way, targeted interventions can address the unique needs of individual clients. Gilgun suggests that prediction of outcomes will be improved by appreciation of the balance or imbalance of risks and assets (see Figure 8.4). The prognosis would likely be best in quadrant B and worst in quadrant C.

Figure 8.3   Elements of Developmental Competency

1. Closeness, trusting, relationship building
2. Handling separation and independence
3. Handling joint decisions and interpersonal conflict
4. Dealing with frustration and unfavorable events
5. Celebrating good things, feeling pleasure
6. Working for delayed gratification
7. Relaxing, playing
8. Cognitive processing through words, symbols, images
9. An adaptive sense of direction and purpose

Source: Strayhorn, J.M. (1988). *The competent child: An approach to psychotherapy and preventive mental health.* New York: Guilford Press.

Figure 8.4   Gilgun's Model of Risks and Assets

A	Low risk Low asset	B	Low risk High asset
C	High risk Low asset	D	High risk High asset

Source: Gilgun, J. F. (1996b, September). *Clinical instruments for children who have sexually inappropriate behavior.* Paper presented at the Symposium on Psychosocial Interventions: Social Work's Contributions, sponsored by the Institute for the Advancement of Social Work Research and the National Institutes of Health, Washington, D.C. Figure reprinted with permission.

Finkelhor (1995) suggests a model for "developmental victimology," which is also congruent with our group's approach. He suggests that two areas of development should be studied: (1) variables that affect children's risk for victimization (e.g., suitability as targets, ability to protect self, environmental factors), and (2) variables that affect children's reactions to victimization (e.g., developmental impacts, cognitive appraisal, expression of symptoms).

Just as the group was preparing this manuscript, one member came across a 1996 article by Cicchetti and Rogosch that capsulized the developmental aspect of our thinking: "The meaning of any one attribute, process, or psychopathological condition needs to be considered in light of the complex matrix" (p. 599). Cicchetti and Rogosch also referred to Strouge and Rutter (1984) regarding a "more person-oriented level of analysis of differential pathways" (p. 598) in defining theories of developmental psychopathology. It is clear that many theorists working outside the specialty of child sexual abuse have much to offer as this journey continues.

Dynamic Processes

The victim-to-victimizer concept (Ryan, 1989) drew parallels from the cycle used in the treatment of sexually abusive youth (Lane & Zamora, 1978, 1984; Ryan et al., 1988) to understand the dynamic process surrounding abusive behaviors. That cycle is used extensively

Figure 8.5   The High-Risk Cycle

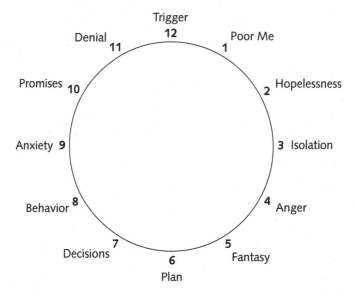

throughout the world as a conceptual framework in the treatment of sexual abusers and has been adapted to many populations (Lane, 1991, 1997; Freeman-Longo & Bays, 1988). The dysfunctional cycle from Chapter 1 has been reframed as a high-risk cycle in work with at-risk children (Ryan & Blum, 1994) as a framework for parents, teachers, caregivers, and therapists to recognize antecedent patterns associated with behaviors that might be harmful to self, others, and/or property (see Figure 8.5). The various elements of this pattern are described, along with possible adult interventions and potential psychiatric features, in Figure 8.6.

The concept of a predictable dynamic process operating as a defensive strategy related to victimization and perpetration issues is the basis for the creation of abuse-specific milieus for treatment of a wide range of behavioral disorders (Ryan, 1997). Recently, Gray (in MacFarlane & Cunningham, 1996) applied the same cyclical pattern to fire-setting behaviors in children with compulsive behavior disorders, helping to demystify a problem that many clinicians had been hesitant to treat. When we are able to see the rationality of the defensive posture clients use to manage stresses that overwhelm their normal coping abilities, it becomes possible to treat a diverse range of problems. The key to changing dysfunctional processes lies in desensitizing overwhelming emotions, creating new skills and options for functioning, and challenging beliefs that support abusive solutions.

One reason that the cycle has been useful for clinicians is that it distinguishes situational, affective, cognitive, and behavioral elements associated with repetitive behaviors. This discrimination enables the therapist to target various elements with psychotherapy, cognitive restructuring, behavior modification, and environmental management using techniques of intervention learned in clinical training. Conditions that resist normal therapeutic interventions can then be targeted through the use of specific techniques indicated by the unique characteristics of the client's life experience, phenomenology, and dynamic processes. One measure of successful treatment may be when high-risk or abusive thoughts are rejected as no longer congruent with the self-image and view of the world (Ryan, 1995).

As presented in Chapter 5, the goal of therapeutic interventions is to mediate potential problems in subsequent functioning. Whether intervening in issues of sexual abuse following a child's immediate disclosure, after a delayed discovery, or in response to negative psychological and/or behavioral sequelae, the goal is to change the course of subsequent functioning. Therapy represents a developmental process.

The therapist offers the therapeutic process as a container for unmanageable issues until the client becomes able to reintegrate painful aspects of life experience as part of a competent and worthy self-image. Therapists must be empathic without being "brainwashed," retaining a clear sense of their own identity without either distancing or losing objectivity. The empathic process does not require the therapist to feel the pain of the client but rather to validate the pain and help the client tolerate memories of earlier life, without being controlled by them, in order to be whole.

A developmental-contextual approach to clients fosters respectful, empathic, and individualized care, restorative habilitation through a new experience of relationship and of the world. The therapist who nurtures growth helps the client move beyond therapy into independence, with the ability to create healthy relationships that are not reminiscent of abusive experiences and to go beyond survival and get on with life.

Figure 8.6 Elements of the High-Risk Cycle

High-Risk Cycle	Adult Interventions	Psychiatric View of Cycle
Trigger: A situation or event evokes a perceived loss of control or lack of safety; feelings of helplessness, frustration, or loss	Help child express sensitive or vulnerable feelings and validate	Flashbacks Flooding Overwhelming affect
Poor Me: Feeling and thinking of self as a victim	Acknowledge that child is feeling unsafe	Victim stance: Paranoia Anxiety Helplessness
Hopelessness: Negative expectations, pessimism, distrust	Challenge beliefs, help child succeed, encourage new experiences, teach skills	Depression External locus of control Disorganized thinking Distortions
Isolation: Alone; no input or feedback	"Be with" the child, offer hugs or sit nearby, listen, do not insist on talking or touching, introduce relaxing distractions such as turning pages in a picture book or magazine	Dissociation Withdrawal Avoidant behavior
Anger: Masks vulnerability; control seeking manifests in power struggles (e.g., manipulation, tantrums, arguments)	Refuse to engage in power struggles; label behavior and emotions; teach anger management (e.g., counting, drawing, time out, exercise); do not offer aggressive outlets such as punching pillows, screaming	Defensiveness Projection Externalizing Mania Hysteria
Fantasy: Imagining solutions: "What will make me feel better?" "How can I get back a sense of control?" "I'll show them how bad it feels!"	Listen attentively and offer self-nurturing or prosocial solutions—a hug, a snack, quiet time, music, games, crafts, assertiveness, exercise, problem solving	Fantasy solution: Ruminating, intrusive thoughts, grandiosity, suicidal ideation, paraphilic ideation, homicidal ideation

Figure 8.6 Elements of the High-Risk Cycle (cont.)

High-Risk Cycle	Adult Interventions	Psychiatric View of Cycle
Plan: What? When? (access, opportunity)	Supervise, prevent, limit access and opportunity	Ritualized Defensive
Decisions: Choice: "I'll do it now."	Accountability for choices (label bad choices; reinforce good choices)	Impulsive Dissociated Irrational
Behaviors: Compensatory, dysfunctional behavior; abusive to self, others, or property (sexually abusive, sexually promiscuous, substance abuse, overeating, food refusal, violence, fire setting, risk taking, suicidal gestures, vandalism)	Label, express your feelings, make a rule, specify consequences and rewards (try to intervene sooner)	Disordered Habituated Reinforcing Aggressive Self-destructive
Anxiety: Uh oh! "What if I get caught?"	Validate feelings, express and validate child's disappointment that the good feelings of the behavior were temporary and didn't last	Attention deficits Distractibility Hypervigilance
Promises: "Never again!"	Help child develop plan to succeed in managing the behavior	Grandiosity Magical bargaining
Denial: "No problem"	Confront distortions, acknowledge risk of behavior recurring	Amnesia Dissociated

Postscript

The study group's process owes its longevity and success to several features of the work:

Collegial Support

The group has continually provided a forum for members to review clinical cases and dilemmas in practice with colleagues in an atmosphere of equality, respect, and trust. This aspect of the group process has been equally important for members who work in private practice, to counter the isolation and insularity of working alone, and for members working in large agencies, where office politics and incestuous dynamics can create the risk of rigid thinking and closed belief systems.

Study

The learning orientation of the group inherently lends support to the expectation that the group is a place to explore the confusing and the unknown. The constant introduction of new articles into the group's review of the literature has provided both the push and the mechanism for members to follow developments in the field. The curiosity driving the group continually posed new questions that reached into topics surrounding, but not specifically about, the abuse issues.

Urgency

The group has continued to feel the urgency associated with the original question because of the inclusion of members treating children and adolescents who have already adopted an abusive lifestyle and adult survivors whose presentation for treatment is testimony to the power, the pain, and the longevity of abuse sequelae. Caseworkers and therapists in the group have been constantly reminded of the relentless intergenerational risks. Children who had been treated as young victims within our own agencies and who resurfaced as adolescents in residential programs or delinquency petition procedures underscore the urgency of this endeavor.

Validation

Members developed a base of common knowledge over time that facilitated the dialogue, and the members' ability to confront discrepancies and dysfunction within the group was both challenging and validating of the risk of parallel process with difficult clients. To meet every month with colleagues who could be trusted and leaned on, when "expertise" proved inadequate and lonely, was a welcome relief, rejuvenating the members' view of the world and of relationships as good and worthy and dependable.

Articulation

The commitment to write about the group's process posed a new challenge to the group and energized its process for over a year. To take pen in hand and commit thoughts and beliefs to paper created a new anxiety. On the one hand, the members' desire to share the process with colleagues was motivated by a belief that because the matrix was so useful to us, others might benefit from it as well. On the other hand, so much of what came to mind in the process seemed mundane or obvious — so simplistic that in preparing for an oral presentation in 1994, the process seemed almost foolish. The enthusiasm of a standing-room-only crowd at that seminar in Keystone, Colorado, combined with the feedback from those attending, reassured the group that others were struggling with issues so similar that the text seemed worthwhile.

The group has spent many hours contemplating the dilemma of young workers in the field, especially line staff in residential milieus who may not be much older than their clients and often have less clinical training than professionals in private practice. The task of modeling healthy human functioning may be difficult for staff who have not completed the developmental tasks with which their clients are struggling and who may have some of the same issues as their client population. Good supervision and training may mitigate the negative impacts of the work, but every therapeutic agent must expect that the work will change him/her. Such changes may be viewed as a threat, a challenge, or an opportunity. Joining in a process of discovery with a group of colleagues can increase the positive effects of the work as well as increase the efficiency of the worker.

We hope that we have conveyed the spirit of our process, as well as some useful thoughts and concerns. We welcome feedback from our colleagues who read this volume and encourage continued curiosity. We are all engaged in a collective process of discovery, and we should remember that the process itself is a valuable component of the work.

—Gail Ryan and Associates

The Kempe Study Group is currently pursuing a better understanding of neurological functioning by studying Fay Honey Knopp's final text, A Primer on the Complexities of Traumatic Memory of Childhood Sexual Abuse *(Knopp and Benson, 1996, Safer Society Press).*

References

Adams-Tucker, C. (1980). *Sex-abused children: Pathology and clinical traits.* Paper presented at the annual meeting of American Psychiatric Association, San Francisco, CA.

Adams-Tucker, C. (1982). Proximate effects of sexual abuse in childhood. *American Journal of Psychiatry, 139*(10), 1252–1256.

Ainsworth, M.D.S. (1985). Attachments across the lifespan. *Bulletin of the New York Academy of Medicine, 61*, 792–812.

Ainsworth, M.D.S., Blehar, M.C., Waters, E., & Wall, S. (1978). *Patterns of attachment: A psychological study of the strange situation.* Hillsdale, NJ: Erlbaum.

Ainsworth, M.D.S., & Wittig, B.A. (1969). Attachment and exploratory behavior of one-year-olds in a strange situation. In B.M. Foss (Ed.), *Determinants of infant behavior IV* (pp. 111–136). London: Methuen & Company.

Alexander, P.C. (1993). The differential effects of abuse characteristics and attachment in the prediction of long term effects of sexual abuse. *Journal of Interpersonal Violence, 8*, 346–362.

Arroyo, W., Eth, S., & Pynoos, R. (1984). Sexual assault of a mother by her pre-adolescent son. *American Journal of Psychiatry, 141*, 1107–1108.

Bagley, C., Wood, N., & Young, L. (1994). Victim to abuser: Mental health and behavioral sequels of child sexual abuse in a community survey of young adult males. *Child Abuse & Neglect, 18*, 683–697.

Becker, J.V. (1988). The effects of child sexual abuse on adolescent sex offenders. In G. E. Wyatt & G.J. Powell (Eds.), *Lasting effects of child sexual abuse* (pp. 193–207). Newbury Park, CA: Sage.

Becker, J., Skinner, L., Abel, G., & Treacy, E. (1982). Incidence of sexual dysfunction in rape and incest victims. *Journal of Sex and Marital Therapy, 8*, 65–74.

Bennett, M. (1979). Overcoming the golden rule: Sympathy and empathy. *Communication Yearbook, 3*, 407–422.

Berliner, L., & Loftus, E. (1992). Sexual abuse accusations: Desperately seeking reconciliation. *Journal of Interpersonal Violence, 7*, 570–578.

Biringen, Z. (1994). Attachment theory and research: Application to clinical practice. *American Journal of Orthopsychiatry, 64*, 404–420.

Blos, P. (1985). Intergenerational separation-individuation. *Psychoanalytic Study of the Child, 40*, 41–50.

155

Blum, J., & Gray, S. (1987, May). *Strategies for communicating with young children.* Seminar presented at the 16th National Symposium on Child Abuse and Neglect, Keystone, CO.

Bolton, F.G., Morris, L.A., & Maceachron, A.E. (1989). *Males at risk: The other side of child sexual abuse.* Newbury Park, CA: Sage.

Bowlby, J. (1969). *Attachment and loss: Vol. 1.* New York: Basic Books.

Bowlby, J. (1980). *Attachment and loss: Vol. 3. Loss: Sadness and depression.* New York: Basic Books.

Bowlby, J. (1985). Violence in the family as a function of the attachment system. *American Journal of Psychoanalysis, 44,* 9–27.

Bowlby, J. (1988). Developmental psychiatry comes of age. *American Journal of Psychiatry, 145,* 1–10.

Brazelton, T.B., & Cramer, B.G. (1990). *The earliest relationship.* New York: Addison-Wesley.

Briere, J. (1990). Denial: The desire not to know. *Preventing Sexual Abuse,* 8–12.

Briere, J., & Runtz, M. (1989). The trauma symptom checklist (TSC-33): Early data on a new scale. *Journal of Interpersonal Violence, 4,* 151–163.

Briere, J., & Runtz, M. (1993). Childhood sexual abuse: Long-term sequelae and implications for psychological assessment. Prepublication draft.

Briggs, D.C. (1975). *Your child's self-esteem.* New York: Doubleday.

Browne, A., & Finkelhor, D. (1986). Initial and long-term effects: A review of the research. In D. Finkelhor (Ed.), *A sourcebook on childhood sexual abuse* (pp. 143–179). Beverly Hills, CA: Sage.

Calderone, M.S. (1983). On the possible prevention of sexual problems in adolescence. *Hospital and Community Psychiatry, 34,* 528–530.

Cantwell, H.B. (1988). Child sexual abuse: Very young perpetrators. *Child Abuse & Neglect, 12,* 579–582.

Cavanaugh-Johnson, T. (1987). Child perpetrators: Children who molest children. *Child Abuse & Neglect, 12,* 219–230.

Chess, S., & Thomas, A. (1984). *Origins and evolution of behavior disorders.* New York: Bruner/Mazel.

Chrestman, K.R. (1994). *Secondary traumatization in therapists working with survivors of trauma.* Unpublished doctoral dissertation, Nova University, Fort Lauderdale, FL.

Christoffel, K.K., & Forsyth, B.W.C. (1989). Mirror image of environmental deprivation: Severe childhood obesity of psychosocial origins. *Child Abuse & Neglect, 13,* 249–256.

Cicchetti, D. (1987). Developmental psychopathology in infancy: Illustration from the study of maltreated youngsters. *Journal of Consulting and Clinical Psychology, 55*(6), 837–845.

Cicchetti, D., & Cummings, E.M. (Eds.). (1990). *Attachment in the pre-school years: Theory, research, and intervention.* Chicago: University of Chicago Press.

Cicchetti, D., & Rogosch, F. (1996). Equifinality and multifinality in developmental psychopathology. *Development and Psychopathology, 8,* 597–600.

Conte, J. (1985a). Clinical dimensions of adult sexual abuse of children. *Behavioral Science and the Law, 3*(4), 341–354.

Conte, J. (1985b). The effects of sexual victimization on children: A critique and suggestions for future research. *Victimology, 10*, 110–130.

Conte, J.R. (1986). Sexual abuse and the family: A critical analysis. In T. Trepper & M. Barrett (Eds.), *Treating incest: A multimodal systems perspective* (pp. 83–97). Boston: Hayworth Press.

Conte, J. (1988). *The effects of sexual abuse on the child victim and its treatment.* Presentation at the 4th national meeting on Child Sexual Abuse, Huntsville, AL.

Crittendon, P. (1992). Children's strategies for coping with adverse home environments: An interpretation using attachment theory. *Child Abuse & Neglect, 16*(3), 330.

Cummings, E.M., & Cicchetti, D. (1990). Toward a transactional model of relations between attachment and depression. In M.T. Greenberg, D. Cicchetti, & E.M. Cummings (Eds.), *Attachment in the preschool years: Theory, research and intervention* (pp. 339–374). Chicago: University of Chicago Press.

Davis, D.L., & Boster, L.H. (1992). Cognitive-behavioral-expressive interventions with aggressive and resistant youths. *Child Welfare, 71*, 557–573.

DeFrancis, V. (1969). *Protecting the child victim of sex crimes committed by adults.* Denver, CO: American Humane Association.

Delaney, R.J. (1991). *Fostering changes.* Fort Collins, CO: Corbett.

DeYoung, M. (1982). Self-injurious behavior in incest victims: A research note. *Child Welfare, 61*, 577–584.

Dodge, K., and Garber, J. (1992). Domains of emotion regulation. In J. Garber & K.A. Dodge (Eds.), *The development of emotion regulation and dysregulation* (pp. 3–11). New York: Cambridge University Press.

Donovan, D., & McIntyre, D. (1990). *Healing the hurt child: A developmental contextual model.* New York: Norton.

Downs, W.R. (1993). Developmental considerations for the effects of childhood sexual abuse. *Journal of Interpersonal Violence, 8*, 331–345.

Egeland, B., & Susman-Tillman, A. (1996). Dissociation as a mediator of child abuse across generations. *Child Abuse & Neglect, 20*, 1123–1132.

Epstein, L., & Feiner, A. (Eds.). (1979). *Countertransference: The therapist's contribution to the therapeutic situation.* New York: Jason Arons.

Erickson, M.F., Korfmacher, J., & Egeland, B.R. (1992). Attachments past and present: Implications for therapeutic intervention with mother/infant diads. *Development and Psychopathology, 4*, 495–507.

Erickson, M.F., Sroufe, L.A., & Egeland, B.R. (1985). A relationship between quality of attachment and behavior problems in preschool in a high-risk sample. In I. Bretherton & E. Waters (Eds.), *Monographs of the Society for Research and Child Development, 50*, 147–166.

Erikson, E. (1959). *Identity and the life cycle.* New York: Norton.

Evans, S., Schaefer, S., & Sterne, M. (1984). *Sexual victimization patterns of recovering chemically dependent women.* Paper presented at the meeting of the International Institute on Prevention and Treatment of Alcoholism, Athens, Greece.

Fagan, J. (1984, October). New evidence links multiple personalities to child abuse. *Children and Teens in Crisis*, p. 12.

Fagan, J., & Wexler, S. (1983). Explanations of assault among violent delinquents. *Journal of Adolescent Research, 13*(3), 363–385.

Farrenkopf, T. (1992). What happens to therapists who work with sex offenders? *Journal of Offender Rehabilitation, 18*, 217–223.

Finkelhor, D. (1986). Initial and long-term effects: A review of the research. In D. Finkelhor (Ed.), *A sourcebook on child sexual abuse* (pp. 143–179). Beverly Hills, CA: Sage.

Finkelhor, D. (1995). The victimization of children: A developmental perspective. *American Journal of Orthopsychiatry, 65*(2).

Finkelhor, D., & Berliner, L. (1995). Research on the treatment of sexually abused children: A review and recommendations. *Journal of the American Academy of Child and Adolescent Psychiatry, 34*(11), 1408–1423.

Finkelhor, D., & Browne, A. (1985). The traumatic impact of child sexual abuse: A conceptualization. *American Journal of Orthopsychiatry, 55*, 530–539.

Finkelhor, D., & Dziuba-Leatherman, J. (1994). Victimization of children. *American Psychologist, 49*, 173–183.

Finkelhor, D., Hotaling, G., Lewis, I.A., & Smith, C. (1990). Sexual abuse in the national survey of adult men and women: Prevalence, characteristics, and risk factors. *Child Abuse & Neglect, 14*, 19–28.

Firestone, R.W. (1990). *The universality of emotional child abuse*. In R.W. Firestone (Ed.), *Compassionate child rearing* (pp. 319–320). New York: Plenum.

Ford, C.S., & Beach, S.A. (1951). Development of sexual behavior in human beings. In R. Grinder (Ed.), *Patterns of sexual behavior* (pp. 433–445). New York: Harper & Brothers.

Fraiberg, S., Adelson, E., & Shapiro, V. (1975). Ghosts in the nursery: A psychoanalytic approach to the problems of impaired mother-infant relationships. *Journal of the American Academy of Child Psychiatry, 14*, 387–421.

Frankl, V. (1984). *Man's search for meaning*. New York: Washington Square Press.

Freeman-Longo, R. (1986). The impact of sexual victimization on males. *Child Abuse & Neglect, 10*, 411–414.

Freeman-Longo, R.E., & Bays, L. (1988). *Who am I and why am I in treatment?* Orwell, VT: Safer Society Press.

Freud, A. (1981). A psychoanalyst's view of sexual abuse by parents. In P.B. Mrazek & C.H. Kempe (Eds.), *Sexually abused children and their families* (pp. 33–34). New York: Pergamon.

Freud, S. (1955). *Beyond the pleasure principle: group psychology and other works: Vol. 18. A standard edition of the complete psychological works*. (James Strachey, Ed. and Trans.). London: Hogarth. (Original work published 1920)

Freud, S. (1896). *The aetiology of hysteria: Vol. 3. A standard edition of the complete psychological works*. (Translation of "Zur Ätiologie der Hysterie," a modified version of the translation by C.M. Baines, 1924.). London: Hogarth. (Original work published 1896)

Freud, S., Breuer, J.J. (1955). *Studies on hysteria: Vol. 2. A standard edition of the complete psychological works*. (James Strachey, Ed. and Trans.). London: Hogarth. (Original work published 1895)

Friedrich, W.N. (1988). Behavior problems in sexually abused children: An adaptational perspective. In G.E. Wyatt & G.J. Powell (Eds.), *Lasting effects of child sexual abuse* (pp. 171–191). Newbury Park, CA: Sage.

Friedrich, W. (1994). Assessing children for the effects of sexual victimization. In J. Briere (Ed.), *Assessing and treating victims of violence* (pp. 17–28). New Directions for Mental Health Services No. 64. San Francisco: Jossey-Bass.

Friedrich, W. (1995). *Psychotherapy with sexually abused boys: An integrated approach*. Thousand Oaks, CA: Sage.

Friedrich, W.N., Grambsch, P., Damon, L., Koverolo, C., Wolfe, V., Hewitt, S., Lang, R., & Broughton, D. (1992). Child sexual behavior inventory: Normative and clinical comparisons. *Psychological Assessment, 4*, 303–311.

Friedrich, W.N., Luecke, W.J., Beilke, R.L., & Place, V. (1992). Psychotherapy outcome of sexually abused boys. *Journal of Interpersonal Violence, 7*, 396–409.

Friedrich, W.N., Urquiza, A.J., & Beilke, R. (1986). Behavioral problems in sexually abused young children. *Journal of Pediatric Psychology, 11*, 47–57.

Furchner, J. (1989). Respecting the child's eye view. *Preventing Sexual Abuse*, 8–12.

Gadpaille, W.J. (1972, January). Understanding your child's sexual growth. *Sexology*, 19–21.

Gadpaille, W.J. (1975a). Adolescent sexuality: A challenge to psychiatrists. *Journal of the American Academy of Psychoanalysis, 3*, 163–177.

Gadpaille, W.J. (1975b, January). *A consideration of two concepts of normality as it applies to adolescent sexuality*. Paper presented at the Colloquium on Behavioral Sciences, Los Angeles, CA.

Gadpaille, W.J. (1975c). *The cycles of sex*. New York: Scribner's.

Gadpaille, W.J. (1978). Psychosexual development tasks imposed by pathologically delayed childhood: A cultural dilemma. In S. Feinstein & P. Giovachini (Eds.), *Adolescent psychiatry: Vol. 6* (pp. 136–155). Chicago: University of Chicago Press.

Gadpaille, W.J. (1983). Innate masculine/feminine traits: Their contributions to conflict. *Journal of the American Academy of Psychoanalysis, 11*, 401–424.

Galambos, N., & Dixon, R. (1984). Adolescent abuse and the development of personal sense of control. *Child Abuse & Neglect, 8*, 285–293.

George, C. (1993, March). *Toward a theory of caregiving*. Paper presented at the biennial meeting of the Society for Research and Child Development, New Orleans, LA.

George, C. (1994, May). *Internal working models of attachment and caregiving: A representational model of child abuse and intervention*. Paper presented at the 21st Annual Symposium on Child Abuse and Neglect, Keystone, CO.

George, C., & Solomon, J. (1989). Internal working models of caregiving and security of attachment at age 6. *Infant Mental Health Journal, 10*, 222–227.

Gil, E., & Johnson, T.C. (1993). *Sexualized children: Assessment and treatment of sexualized children and children who molest*. Rockville, MD: Launch Press.

Gilgun, J. (1988). *Factors which block the development of sexually abusive behavior in adults abused as children.* Paper presented at the national conference of the University of Minnesota Department of Social Work, Minneapolis, MN.

Gilgun, J. (1996). *Human development and adversity in ecological perspective: Part I and II. Families in society.* Manuscript submitted for publication.

Gilgun, J., & Connor, T. (1989). Isolation and the adult male perpetrator of child sexual abuse. Unpublished manuscript.

Goldstein, A. (1987). New directions in aggression reduction. In R. Hinde & J. Groebel (Eds.), *Aggression and war: Biological and social basis* (pp. 97–132). Cambridge, England: Cambridge University Press.

Gomes-Schwartz, B., Horowitz, J.M., & Cardarelli, A.P. (Eds.). (1990). *Child sexual abuse: The initial effects.* Newbury Park, CA: Sage.

Goodwin, J., Simms, M., & Bergman, R. (1979). Hysterical seizures: A sequel to incest. *American Journal of Orthopsychiatry, 49,* 698–703.

Gordon, B.N., Schroeder, C.S., & Abrams, J.N. (1990). Children's knowledge of sexuality: A comparison of sexually abused and non-abused children. *American Journal of Orthopsychiatry, 60,* 250–257.

Groth, N., & Birnbaum, J. (1978). Adult sexual orientation and attraction to underage persons. *Archives of Sexual Behavior, 7*(3), 175–181.

Groth, N., & Longo, R. (1979). *Men who rape: The psychology of the offender.* New York: Plenum.

Harter, S. (1983). Cognitive-developmental considerations in play therapy. In C. Schaefer & L. O'Connor (Eds.), *Handbook of play therapy* (pp. 94–127). New York: John Wiley & Sons.

Hartman, C.R., & Burgess, A.W. (1993). Information processing of trauma. *Child Abuse & Neglect, 17,* 47–58.

Haynes-Seman, C. (1985, May). *Review of the literature on child abuse and neglect.* Presentation at the 14th National Symposium on Child Abuse and Neglect, Keystone, CO.

Haynes-Seman, C. (1987, May). *Impact of sexualized attention on the preverbal child.* Presentation at the 16th National Symposium on Child Abuse and Neglect, Keystone, CO.

Haynes-Seman, C. (1989). Sexualized attention: Normal interactional or precursor to sexual abuse. *American Journal of Orthopsychiatry, 59,* 238–245.

Haynes-Seman, C.F., & Hart, J.S. (1988). Interactional assessment: Evaluation of parent-child relationships in abuse and neglect. In D.C. Bross, R.B. Krugman, N.R. Lenherr, D.A. Rosenberg, & B.D. Schmidt (Eds.), *The new child protection team handbook* (pp. 181–198). New York: Garland.

Haynes-Seman, C.F., & Kelly, M. (1988). Disturbed parent-infant relationships. *Colorado Psychological Association Bulletin,* 5–7.

Herman, J. (1992). *Trauma and recovery: The aftermath of violence — from domestic abuse to political terror.* New York: Basic Books.

Hindman, J. (1989). *Just before dawn: From the shadows of tradition to new reflections in trauma assessment and treatment of sexual victimization.* Ontario, OR: Alex-Andria Associates.

Hiroto, D. (1974). Locus of control and learned helplessness. *Journal of Experimental Psychology, 102*(2), 187–193.

Hunter, J.A. (1996). *Working with children and adolescents who sexually abuse children*. Paper presented at the 11th International Congress on Child Abuse and Neglect, Dublin, Ireland. Reporting on Federal Grant No. 90-CA-1454.

Hunter, J.A., & Becker, J. (1994). The role of deviant arousal in juvenile sexual offending: Etiology, evaluation and treatment. *Criminal Justice and Behavior, 21*(4).

Isaac, C. (1987, May). *Identification and interruption of sexually offending behaviors in prepubescent children*. Presentation at the 16th National Symposium on Child Abuse and Neglect, Keystone, CO.

Janoff-Bulman, R. (1992). *Shattered assumptions: Toward a new psychology of trauma*. New York: Free Press.

Jenkins, A. (1990). *Invitation to responsibility*. Adelaide, Australia: Dulwich Centre.

Johnson, B.K., & Kenkel, M.B. (1991). Stress, coping, and adjustment in female adolescent incest victims. *Child Abuse & Neglect, 15*, 293–305.

Johnson, T.C. (1988). Child perpetrators — children who molest other children: Preliminary findings. *Child Abuse & Neglect, 12*, 219–229.

Johnson, T.C. (1991, August/September). Understanding the sexual behaviors of young children. *SIECUS Report*, 8–15.

Johnson, T.C., & Berry, C. (1989). Children who molest: A treatment program. *Journal of Interpersonal Violence, 4*, 185–203.

Karen, R. (1990, February). Becoming attached. *Atlantic Monthly*, pp. 35–71.

Karen, R. (1994). *Becoming attached*. New York: Warner.

Katz, M. (1997). *On playing a poor hand well: Insights from the lives of those who have overcome childhood risks and adversities*. New York: Norton.

Kaufman, J., & Zigler, E. (1987). Do abused children become abusive parents? *American Journal of Orthopsychiatry, 57*, 186–192.

Kempe, C.H., & Helfer, R.E. (1980). *The battered child* (3rd ed). Chicago: University of Chicago Press.

Kempe, C.H., Silverman, F.N., Steele, B.F., Droegemueller, W., & Silver, H.K. (1966). The battered-child syndrome. *Journal of the American Medical Association, 181*(1), 17–24.

Kempe, R.S., & Kempe, C.H. (1984). *The common secret*. New York: W.H. Freeman.

Kendall-Tackett, K.A., Williams, L.M., & Finkelhor, D. (1993). Impact of sexual abuse on children: A review and synthesis of recent empirical studies. *Psychological Bulletin, 113*(1), 164–180.

Kline, D.F. (1987). *Long term impact of child maltreatment on the victims as reflected in further contact with the Utah Juvenile Court and the Utah Department of Adult Corrections*. Logan, UT: Utah State University.

Korbin, J. (1987). Child maltreatment in cross-cultural perspective: Vulnerable children and circumstances. In R. Gelles & J. Lancaster (Eds.), *Child abuse and neglect: Biosocial dimensions* (pp. 31–55). New York: Aldine de Gruyter.

Krugman, R. (1987). The assessment process of a child protection team. In R. Helfer & R. Kempe (Eds.), *The battered child* (pp. 127–136). Chicago: University of Chicago Press.

Kurtz, H. (1984). The effects of victimization on acceptance of aggression and the expectations of assertive traits in children as measured by the general social survey. *Victimology, 9*(1), 166–173.

Lamb, S., & Edgar-Smith, S. (1994). Aspects of disclosure: Mediators of outcome of childhood sexual abuse. *Journal of Interpersonal Violence, 9*, 307–326.

Landry, S., & Peters, R.D. (1992). Toward understanding of a developmental paradigm for aggressive conduct problems during the preschool years. In R.D. Peters, R. McMahon, & V. Quinsey (Eds.), *Aggression and violence throughout the lifespan* (pp. 1–30). Newbury Park, CA: Sage.

Lane, S. (1991). Special offender populations. In G.D. Ryan & S.L. Lane (Eds.), *Juvenile sexual offending: Causes, consequences and correction* (pp. 299–332). Lexington, MA: Lexington Books.

Lane, S. (1997). The sexual abuse cycle. In G. Ryan & S. Lane (Eds.), *Juvenile sexual offending: Causes, consequences and correction* (2nd ed., pp. 77–121). San Francisco: Jossey-Bass.

Lane, S., & Zamora, P. (1978). [Syllabus materials from in-service training on adolescent sex offenders, Closed Adolescent Treatment Center, Division of Youth Services, Denver, CO.] Unpublished.

Lane, S., & Zamora, P. (1984). A method for treating the adolescent sex offender. In R. Mathias, P. Demuro, & R. Allinson (Eds.), *Violent juvenile offenders*. San Francisco: National Council on Crime and Delinquency.

Law, S. (1987). [Clinical notes from client interviews.] Unpublished raw data.

Laws, D.R., & Marshall, W.L. (1990). A conditioning theory of the etiology and maintenance of deviant sexual preference and behavior. In W.L. Marshall, D.R. Laws, & H.E. Barbaree (Eds.), *Handbook of sexual assault: Issues, theories and treatment of the offender* (pp. 209–229). New York: Plenum Press.

Lieberman, A.F. (1996). Aggression and sexuality in relation to toddler attachment: Implications for the caregiving system. *Infant Mental Health Journal, 17*(3), 276–292.

Lieberman, A.F., & Paul, J.H. (1990). Disorders of attachment and secure base behavior in the second year of life: Conceptual issues and clinical intervention. In M.T. Greenberg, D. Cicchetti, & E.M. Cummings (Eds.), *Attachment in the pre-school years: Theory, research, and intervention* (pp. 375–398). Chicago: University of Chicago Press.

Lindberg, F.H., & Distad, L.J. (1985). Survival responses to incest: Adolescents in crisis. *Child Abuse & Neglect, 9*, 521–526.

Lipovsky, J.A., Saunders, B.E., & Murphy, S.N. (1989). Depression, anxiety, and behavioral problems among victims of father-child sexual assault and non-abused siblings. *Journal of Interpersonal Violence, 4*, 452–468.

Longo, R. (1982). Sexual learning and experience among adolescent sexual offenders. *International Journal of Offender Therapy and Comparative Criminology, 26*(3), 235–241.

Lynch, M. (1985). Child abuse before Kempe: An historical literature review. *Child Abuse & Neglect, 9*(1), 7–15.

MacFarlane, K., & Cunningham, C. (1996). *When children abuse: Group treatment strategies for children with impulse control problems.* Brandon, VT: Safer Society.

Mahler, M.S., Pine, F., & Bergman, A. (1975). *The psychological birth of the human infant: Symbiosis and individuation.* New York: Basic Books.

Main, M., & Solomon, J. (1990). Procedures for identifying infants as disorganized/disoriented during the Ainsworth Strange Situation. In M.T. Greenberg, D. Cicchetti, & E.M. Cummings (Eds.), *Attachment in the pre-school years: Theory, research, and intervention* (pp. 121–160). Chicago: University of Chicago Press.

Mangelsdorf, S., Gunnar, M., Kestenbaum, R., Lang, S., & Andreas, D. (1990). Infant proneness-to-distress, temperament, maternal personality, and mother-infant attachment: Associations and goodness of fit. *Child Development, 61,* 820–831.

Mann, E., & McDermott, J. (1983). Play therapy for victims of child abuse and neglect. In C. Schaefer & L. O'Conner (Eds.), *Handbook of play therapy* (pp. 284–307). New York: John Wiley & Sons.

Mannarino, A.P., Cohen, J.A., & Gregor, N. (1989). Emotional and behavioral difficulties in sexually abused girls. *Journal of Interpersonal Violence, 4,* 437–451.

Marshall, W.L., & Barbaree, H.E. (1990). An integrated theory of the etiology of sexual offending. In W.L. Marshall, D.R. Laws, & H.E. Barbaree (Eds.), *Handbook of sexual assault: Issues, theories and treatment of the offender* (pp. 257–275). New York: Plenum Press.

Marshall, W.L., Hudson, S.N., & Hodkinson, S. (1993). The importance of attachment bonds and the development of juvenile sex offending. In H.E. Barbaree, W.L. Marshall, & S.M. Hudson (Eds.), *The juvenile sex offender* (pp. 164–181). New York: Guilford.

Marshall, W.L., Hudson, S.N., Jones, R., & Fernandez, Y.N. (1994). Empathy in sex offenders. *Clinical Psychology Review, 15,* 99–113.

Marshall, W.L., & Mazzucco, A. (1995). Self-esteem and parental attachments in child molesters. *Sexual Abuse: A Journal of Research and Treatment, 7*(4), 279–286.

Maslow, A. (1964). *Toward a psychology of being.* New York: Van Nostrand.

McCann, L., & Pearlman, L.A. (1990). Vicarious traumatization: The emotional process of working with survivors. *Treating Abuse Today, 3,* 28–31.

McLeer, S., Deblinger, E., Atkins, M., Foa, E., & Ralphe, D. (1988). Post-traumatic stress disorder in sexually abused children. *Journal of the American Academy of Child and Adolescent Psychiatry, 27,* 650–654.

Miller, A. (1990). *The untouched key: Tracing childhood trauma in creativity and destructiveness.* (H. Hannum & H. Hannum, Trans.). New York: Doubleday. (Original work published 1988)

Morris, L.G., & Bolton, F.G. (1986). *Males at risk.* Newbury, CA: Sage.

Mrazek, P., & Kempe, H. (1981). *Sexually abused children and their families.* Oxford, England: Pergamon.

Mrazek, P.J., & Mrazek, D.A. (1987). Resilience in child maltreatment victims: A conceptual exploration. *Child Abuse & Neglect, 11*, 357–366.

Nagel, D.E., Putman, F.W., Noll, J.G., & Trickett, P.K. (1997). Disclosure patterns of sexual abuse and psychological functioning at a 1-year follow up. *Child Abuse & Neglect, 21*, 137–149.

National Task Force on Juvenile Sexual Offending. (1988). Preliminary report. *Juvenile & Family Court Journal, 39*(2), 1–67.

Oates, R.K., O'Toole, B.I., Lynch, D.L., Stern, A., & Cooney, G. (1994). Stability and change in outcomes for sexually abused children. *Journal of the American Academy of Child and Adolescent Psychiatry, 33*, 945–953.

Oates, R., Peacock, A., & Forrest, D. (1985). Long term effects of non-organic failure to thrive. *Pediatrics, 75*(1), 36–40.

Oppenheimer, R., Howells, K., Palmer, R.L., & Challoner, D.A. (1985). *Adverse sexual experience and clinical eating disorders: A preliminary description.* Unpublished manuscript, University of Leicester, United Kingdom.

Ornstein, A. (1991a, April). *The diagnostic therapeutic interview: Conceptual framework and clinical implications.* Paper presented at the Rosenberry Conference, Denver, CO.

Ornstein, A. (1991b, April). *Parental empathy, parental self-object functions and the assessment of parental dysfunction.* Paper presented at the Rosenberry Conference, Denver, CO.

Paperny, D.M., & Deisher, R.W. (1983). Maltreatment of adolescents: The relationship to a predisposition toward violent behavior and delinquency. *Adolescence, 18*, 499–506.

Partridge, S.E. (1988). The parental self-concept: A theoretical exploration and practical application. *American Journal of Orthopsychiatry, 58*, 281–287.

Perry, B.D. (1993). Neurodevelopment and the neurophysiology of trauma: Conceptual considerations for clinical work with maltreated children. *APSAC Advisor, 6*(2), 1, 14–19.

Peters, R.D., McMahon, R.J., & Quinsey, V. (1992). *Aggression and violence throughout the life span.* Newbury Park, CA: Sage.

Peterson, A.L.T. (1992, May–June). Sibling sexual abuse: Emerging awareness of an ignored childhood trauma. *Moving Forward, 1*, 12–13.

Pithers, W.D. (1994). Process evaluation of a group therapy component designed to enhance sex offenders' empathy for sexual abuse survivors. *Behavioral Research and Therapy, 32*, 565–570.

Prentky, R., Knight, R., Straus, H., Rokou, F., Cerce, D., & Sims-Knight, J. (1989). Developmental antecedents of sexual aggression. *Development and Psychopathology, 1*, 153–169.

Radke-Yarrow, M., McCann, K., DeMulder, E., Belmont, B., Martinez, P., & Richardson, D.T. (1995). Attachment in the context of high-risk conditions. *Development and Psychopathology, 7*, 247–265.

Rasmussen, L.A., Burton, J.E., & Christopherson, B.M. (1992). Precursors to offending and the trauma outcome process in sexually reactive children. *Journal of Child Sexual Abuse, 1*, 33–48.

Roesler, T.A., Riggs, S., Alareo, A.J., & McHorney, C. (1990). Health risk behaviors and attempted suicide in adolescents who report prior maltreatment. *Journal of Pediatrics, 116,* 815–820.

Root, M.P.P. (1989). Treatment failures: The role of sexual victimization in women's addictive behavior. *American Journal of Orthopsychiatry, 59,* 542–549.

Ross, R. (1996, November). *ADHD: Why treat at all?* Presentation at ADHD Parent Association Conference, Denver, CO.

Ryan, G. (1981). *The threshold of nurturance: A fundamental difference among abusive families.* Unpublished manuscript.

Ryan, G. (1984, January). The child abuse connection. *Interchange,* 1–4.

Ryan, G. (1989). Victim to victimizer: Rethinking victim treatment. *Journal of Interpersonal Violence, 4,* 325–341.

Ryan, G. (1995, September). *Treatment of sexually abusive youth: The evolving consensus.* Paper presented at the International Experts Conference, Utrecht, Netherlands.

Ryan, G. (1997). The sexual abuser. In M. Helfer, R. Kempe, & R. Krugman (Eds.), *The battered child,* (5th ed., pp. 329–345). Chicago: University of Chicago Press.

Ryan, G., & Blum, J. (1994). *Childhood sexuality: A guide for parents.* Denver, CO: Kempe Center, University of Colorado Health Sciences Center.

Ryan, G., Blum, J., Laws, S., Christopher, D., Weher, F., Sundine, D., Astler, L., Teske, J., & Dale, J. (1988). *Understanding and responding to the sexual behavior of children: Trainer's manual.* Denver, CO: Kempe National Center, University of Colorado Health Sciences Center.

Ryan, G., & Lane, S. (1991). The impact of sexual abuse on the interventionist. In G.D. Ryan & S.L. Lane (Eds.), *Juvenile sexual offending: Causes, consequences and correction* (pp. 411–428). Lexington, MA: Lexington Books.

Ryan, G., & Lane, S. (Eds.). (1997). *Juvenile sexual offending: Causes, consequences and correction* (2nd ed.). Los Angeles, CA: Jossey-Bass.

Ryan, G., Lane, S., Davis, J., & Isaac, C. (1987). Juvenile sexual offenders: Development and correction. *Child Abuse & Neglect, 2,* 385–395.

Ryan, G., Miyoshi, T., Metzner, J., Krugman, R., & Fryer, G. (1996). Trends in a national sample of sexually abusive youths. *Journal of the American Academy of Child and Adolescent Psychiatry, 35*(1), 17–25.

Sanford, L. (1987). Pervasive fears in victims of sexual abuse: A clinician's observations. *Preventing Sexual Abuse, 2*(2), 3–5.

Sauzier, N. (1990). The aftermath of child sexual abuse: 18 months later. In B. Gomez-Schwartz, J.M. Horowitz, & A. Cadarelli (Eds.), *Child sexual abuse: The initial effects* (pp. 132–151). Newbury Park, CA: Sage.

Schrut, A. (1989). *Parent-child interaction and the development of gender identity and sexual partner choice.* Unpublished manuscript.

Seman, C.H. (1994, March). *Attachment and treatment issues: Addressing the problem and not the symptoms.* Paper presented at the 6th annual conference on Child Abuse Prevention, Orange County, CA.

Sigafoos, A.D., Feinstein, C.B., Damond, M., & Reiss, D. (1988). *Measurement of behavioral autonomy in adolescents: The autonomous functioning checklist.* Chicago: University of Chicago Press.

Silvern, L., & Kaersvang, L. (1989). The traumatized children of violent marriages. *Child Welfare, 68*, 421–436.

Solomon, J., & George, C. (1991, April). *Symbolic representation of attachment in children classified as controlling at age 6: Evidence of disorganization of representation strategies.* Paper presented at the meeting of Society for Research in Child Development, Seattle, WA.

Spiegel, D. (Ed.) (1993). *Dissociative disorders: A clinical review.* Lutherville, MD: Sidran Press.

Spitz, R.A. (1945). Hospitalism: An inquiry into the genesis of psychiatric conditions in early childhood. *Psychoanalytic Study of the Child, 1*, 53–74.

Steele, B. (1986). Notes on the lasting effects of early child abuse throughout the life cycle. *Child Abuse & Neglect, 10*, 283–291.

Steele, B.F. (1987a). Abuse and neglect in the earliest years: Groundwork for vulnerability. *Zero to Three, 7*(4), 14–15.

Steele, B. (1987b). Psychodynamic factors in child abuse. In R. Helfer & R. Kempe (Eds.), *The battered child* (pp. 127–136). Chicago: University of Chicago Press.

Steele, B.F. (1989, May). *Variations on a theme of attachment.* Paper presented at the 16th National Symposium on Child Abuse and Neglect, Keystone, CO.

Steele, B.F. (1990, May). *Treating people, not labeled.* Paper presented at the 17th National Symposium on Child Abuse and Neglect, Keystone, CO.

Steele, B.F. (1991). The psychopathology of incest participants. In S. Kramer & S. Akhtar (Eds.), *The trauma of transgression: Psychotherapy of incest victims* (pp. 13–37). Northvale, NJ: Jason Aronson.

Steele, B.F. (1994). Psychoanalysis and the maltreatment of children. *Journal of the American Psychoanalytic Association, 42*, 1001–1025.

Stern, D. (1985). *The interpersonal world of the infant.* New York: Basic Books.

Stovall, G., & Craig, R.J. (1990). Mental representations of physically and sexually abused latency-aged females. *Child Abuse & Neglect, 14*(2), 233–234.

Strayhorn, J.M. (1988). *The competent child: An approach to psychotherapy and preventive mental health.* New York: Guilford Press.

Strouge, L.A., & Rutter, M. (1984). The domain of developmental psychopathology. *Child Development, 55*, 17–29.

Summit, R. (1983). The child sexual abuse accommodation syndrome. *Child Abuse & Neglect, 7*(2), 177–193.

Tauber, E.S. (1979). Countertransference reexamined. In L. Epstein & A. Feiner (Eds.), *Countertransference: The therapist's contribution to the therapeutic situation* (pp. 57–67). Northvale, NJ: Jason Aronson.

Terr, L.C. (1983a). Chowchilla revisited: The effects of psychic trauma four years after a school-bus kidnapping. *American Journal of Psychiatry, 140*, 1543–1550.

Terr, L.C. (1983b). Play therapy and psychic trauma: A preliminary report. In C. Schaefer & K. O'Conner (Eds.), *Handbook of play therapy* (pp. 308–319). New York: John Wiley & Sons.

Terr, L. (1988). What happens to the memories of early childhood trauma? *Journal of American Academy of Child and Adolescent Psychiatry, 27,* 96–104.

Terr, L. (1990a, May). *Children's responses to the* Challenger *disaster.* Paper presented at the annual meeting of the American Psychiatric Association, Washington, DC.

Terr, L. (1990b). *Too scared to cry: Psychic trauma in childhood.* New York: Harper & Row.

Terr, L. (1991). Childhood traumas: An outline and overview. *American Journal of Psychiatry, 148*(1), 10–20.

Terr, L. (1994). *Unchained memories.* New York: Basic Books.

Thomas, A., & Chess, S. (1977). *Temperament and development.* New York: Brunner/Mazel.

Timnick, L. (1985, August 25). The *Times* poll. *Los Angeles Times.*

Valliere, P.M., Bybee, D., & Mowbray, C.T. (1988, April). *Using the Achenbach Child Behavior Checklist in child sexual abuse research: Longitude and comparative analyses.* Presentation at the National Symposium on Child Victimization, Anaheim, CA.

van der Kolk, B.A. (Ed.) (1987). *Psychological trauma.* Washington, DC: American Psychiatric Press.

van der Kolk, B., & Greenberg, M.S. (1987). The psychobiology of the trauma response: Hyperarousal, constriction, and addiction to traumatic reexposure. In B.A. Van der Kolk (Ed.), *Psychological Trauma* (pp. 63–88). Washington, DC: American Psychiatric Press.

Ward, T., Hudson, S.M., & Marshall, W.L. (1996). Attachment style in sex offenders: A preliminary study. *Journal of Sex Research, 33*(1), 17–26.

Ward, T., Hudson, S.M., Marshall, W.L., & Siegert, R. (1995). Attachment style and intimacy deficits in sexual offenders: A theoretical framework. *Sexual Abuse: A Journal of Research and Treatment, 7*(4), 317–335.

Ward, T., McCormack, J., & Hudson, S.M. (1997). Sexual offenders' perceptions of their intimate relationships. *Sexual Abuse: A Journal of Research and Treatment, 9*(1), 57–74.

Weiss, J., Rogers, E., Darwin, M., & Dutton, C. (1955). A study of girl sex victims. *Psychiatric Quarterly, 29,* 1–27.

Weissman-Wind, T. (1994). Telling the secret: Adult women describe their disclosures of incest. *Journal of Interpersonal Violence, 9,* 327–338.

Werner, E.E. (1989, April). Children of the garden island. *Scientific American,* 106–111.

Widom, C.S. (1992). *The cycle of violence.* Washington, DC: National Institute of Justice.

Widom, C.S. (1996). Childhood sexual abuse and its criminal consequences. *Society, 33*(4), 47–53.

Widom, C.S., & Williams, L. (1996). *Cycle of sexual abuse. Research inconclusive about whether child victims become adult abusers.* Report to House of Representatives, Committee of Judiciary, Subcommittee on Crime. General Accounting Office, Washington, DC.

Williams, L.M. (1995). *Juvenile and adult offending behavior and other outcomes in a cohort of sexually abused boys: Twenty years later.* Philadelphia: Joseph J. Peters Institute.

Willock, B. (1983). Play therapy with the aggressive, acting-out child. In C. Schaefer & K. O'Conner (Eds.), *Handbook of play therapy* (pp.128–153). New York: John Wiley & Sons.

Wilson, P.W., & Lindy, J.D. (1994). *Countertransference in the treatment of PTSD.* New York: Guilford Press.

Winnicott, D.W. (1972). *The maturational process and the facilitating environment.* Madison, CT: International Universities Press.

Woodling, B., & Kossoris, P. (1981). Sexual misuse: Rape, molestation and incest. *Pediatric Clinics of North America, 28*(2), 481–499.

Yates, A. (1987). Psychological damage associated with extreme eroticism in young children. *Psychiatric Annals, 17,* 257–261.

Young, L. (1992). Sexual abuse and the problem of embodiment. *Child Abuse & Neglect, 16*(1), 89–100.

Young, R.E., Bergandi, T.A., & Titus, T.G. (1994). Comparison of the effects of sexual abuse on male and female latency-aged children. *Journal of Interpersonal Violence, 9,* 291–306.

Contributors

Gail Ryan, M.A., is a program director at the C. Henry Kempe National Center for the Prevention and Treatment of Child Abuse and Neglect, with a faculty appointment in the Department of Pediatrics, University of Colorado Medical School. She has worked at the Kempe Center since 1975, has worked with abusive parents and abused children, and since 1984 has been treating 11- to 17-year-old-males who have molested children. Her primary interest is in the correlation between early life experience and dysfunctional behavior, with an emphasis on prevention of the development of sexually abusive behavior in high-risk groups. She is director of the Perpetration Prevention Program, facilitator of the National Adolescent Perpetration Network, facilitator of the National Task Force on Juvenile Sexual Offending 1986–1993, coordinator of the Perpetration Prevention Treatment Group, and clinical specialist for the Kempe Center's national resource center. She is an experienced trainer and has published widely in the field, coediting the textbook *Juvenile Sexual Offending: Causes, Consequences and Correction* (1991 and 1997) and *Childhood Sexuality: A Guide for Parents* (1994).

Lynda Arnold, L.C.S.W., is in private practice in Denver, Colorado. She has worked in the area of abuse, neglect, and exploitation for the past 22 years. Much of her time has been spent working in Social Services settings. Her primary interest is sexual abuse treatment, and for nine years she worked on a specialized sexual abuse treatment team in a county social services department. In that program, which she helped develop, she provided treatment to sex offenders, nonoffending parents, and children. The program received a national award for being innovative and creative in meeting the needs of the community. She has given numerous pre-

169

sentations to the public and private sectors and is recognized as an expert court witness in sexual abuse cases. She has served on several boards, including the Domestic Violence Certification Board for Adams County.

Tim Fuente, M.S.W., is a licensed clinical social worker in private psychotherapy practice. He has 18 years of clinical experience treating survivors of child sexual abuse and incest, as well as treating sexual abusers with offense-specific therapy. He has served as an expert witness in the justice system for the state of Colorado. He specializes in the treatment of very young children and also treats adolescents and adults in individual, family, marital, and group therapy. His clinical experience includes a wide range of dissociative disorders from post-traumatic stress disorder to dissociated identity disorder. He also provides consultation, training, and supervision to professional individuals, organizations, and agencies.

Gizane Indart, M.A., was trained and educated at Children's Hospital in Buenos Aires, Argentina. She received her master's degree in clinical child psychology in 1987. From 1987 to 1991, she served as training director of the Residency in Clinical Child Psychology, supervising residents in psychology and psychiatry. She moved to Colorado in 1991 and worked as treatment coordinator at the Namaqua Center, a residential and day treatment facility for emotionally disturbed children. In addition, she has helped develop a variety of therapeutic preschool programs for high-risk children. Her primary interests are the link between developmental psychopathology and child maltreatment and the treatment of sexually abusive behaviors in high-risk children. She has presented on child abuse and neglect, attachment, and the treatment of sexually abusive children at local, state, national, and international conferences. She also serves as outside consultant for the Child Protection Team of Children's Hospital in Buenos Aires. She has been a member of the study group since 1992.

Ruth Kempe, M.D., is professor emeritus, Department of Psychiatry, University of Colorado Medical Center; psychiatric consultant to the Kempe National Center; and author of numerous chapters and articles on child abuse and neglect.

Laurie Knight, B.A., supervises the Children's Sexual Abuse Treatment Team of a county department of social services. She has specialized in the assessment and treatment of incest since 1981 and was instrumental in developing the department's first incest treatment team. She has treated victims and offenders of all ages, nonoffending parents, and families in which incest has occurred. She has been a member of the study group since 1989, has served on various community boards and committees, and has presented on the topic of incest at local, state, and national conferences. She is an expert witness in the justice system for the state of Colorado. Her interests focus primarily on developing and implementing compassionate, effective, comprehensive treatment with the goal of an integrated community approach to intervention.

Barry R. Lindstrom, Ph.D., is a licensed clinical psychologist and certified school psychologist. He is the clinical director of the Namaqua Center, a residential and day treatment facility in Loveland, Colorado. He has worked with severely disturbed and abused children and their families since he graduated from Loyola University of Chicago. His primary interest is in the relationship between developmental psychopathology and child abuse. He maintains a private practice that specializes in clinical child psychology and consults with local departments of social services and the courts regarding child abuse and neglect. He has been a member of the study group for eight years and has served on several mental health boards. He has lectured on the topics of child abuse and neglect, attachment, and post-traumatic stress disorder.

Courtney Pullen, M.A., L.P.C., has been in private practice for 13 years. He specializes in the areas of male sexual abuse survivors, post-traumatic stress disorder, men's issues, and relationship issues. He is cofounder and creator of the clinical model for MASA (Males Affected by Sexual Abuse). He has given numerous presentations in the areas of domestic violence and male survivors and is an instructor at the University of Colorado at Denver and a clinical associate in the Graduate School of Professional Psychology at Denver University.

Brandt Steele, M.D., is professor emeritus, Department of Psychiatry, University of Colorado Medical Center; psychiatric consultant to the Kempe National Center; honorary adviser to the National Task Force on Juvenile Sexual Offending; and author of numerous chapters and articles on child abuse and neglect. He has been a mentor to all the clinical programs at the Kempe Center since its beginning and a member of the study group since its inception.

Sherri Wand, M.S.W., is a licensed clinical social worker and has been in private practice for 16 years treating children, adults, and families. She has extensive experience treating survivors of incest and sexual abuse of all ages. She also has experience treating adult sex offenders and has served as an expert witness for the state of Colorado. She has provided training on these topics to a variety of agencies and has presented her work at conferences on child sexual abuse.

Jerry Yager, Psy.D., is a licensed clinical psychologist. He is currently the program director for the Residential Program at Denver Children's Home. He has worked there since 1986 doing individual, group, and family therapies and supervising milieu programming. He also supervises doctorate- and master's-level clinicians in the treatment of traumatized adolescents. Previously, he spent one year at Child and Family Services in Hartford, Connecticut, and five years at the Grant Center in Miami, Florida, as a treatment leader working with children and adolescents.

Select Safer Society Publications

Roadmaps to Recovery: A Guided Workbook for Young People in Treatment by Timothy J. Kahn (1999). $18.

Feeling Good Again by Burt Wasserman (1999). A treatment workbook for boys and girls ages 6 and up who have been sexually abused. $18.

Feeling Good Again Parents & Therapists Guide by Burt Wasserman (1999). $8.

Female Sexual Abusers: Three Views by Patricia Davin, Ph.D., Teresa Dunbar, Ph.D., & Julia Hislop, Ph.D. (1999). $22.

Cultural Diversity in Sexual Abuser Treatment: Issues and Approaches edited by Alvin Lewis, Ph.D. (1999). $22.

Sexual Abuse in America: Epidemic of the 21st Century by Robert E. Freeman-Longo & Geral T. Blanchard (1998). $20.

Personal Sentence Completion Inventory by L.C. Miccio-Fonseca, Ph.D. (1998). $50, includes 10 inventories and user's guide. Additional inventories available in packs of 25 for $25.

When You Don't Know Who to Call: A Consumer's Guide to Selecting Mental Health Care by Nancy Schaufele & Donna Kennedy (1998). $15.

Tell It Like It Is: A Resource for Youth in Treatment by Alice Tallmadge with Galyn Forster (1998). $15.

Back on Track: Boys Dealing with Sexual Abuse by Leslie Bailey Wright & Mindy Loiselle (1997). $14. A workbook for boys ages 10 and up. Foreword by David Calof.

Assessing Sexual Abuse: A Resource Guide for Practitioners edited by Robert Prentky & Stacey Bird Edmunds (1997). $20.

Impact: Working with Sexual Abusers edited by Stacey Bird Edmunds (1997). $15.

Supervision of the Sex Offender by Georgia Cumming & Maureen Buell (1997). $25.

STOP! Just for Kids: For Kids with Sexual Touching Problems adapted by Terri Allred & Gerald Burns from original writings of children in a treatment program (1997). $15.

A Primer on the Complexities of Traumatic Memories of Childhood Sexual Abuse: A Psychobiological Approach by Fay Honey Knopp & Anna Rose Benson (1997). $25.

The Last Secret: Daughters Sexually Abused by Mothers by Bobbie Rosencrans (1997). $20.

Men & Anger: Understanding and Managing Your Anger for a Much Better Life by Murray Cullen & Robert Freeman-Longo. Revised and updated, new self-esteem chapter (1996). $15.

When Children Abuse: Group Treatment Strategies for Children with Impulse Control Problems by Carolyn Cunningham & Kee MacFarlane (1996). $28.

Adolescent Sexual Offender Assessment Packet by Alison Stickrod Gray & Randy Wallace (1992). $8.

The Relapse Prevention Workbook for Youth in Treatment by Charlene Steen (1993). $15.

Pathways: A Guided Workbook for Youth Beginning Treatment by Timothy J. Kahn (Revised Edition 1997). $15.

Pathways Guide for Parents of Youth Beginning Treatment by Timothy J. Kahn (Revised Edition 1997). $8.

Man-to-Man, When Your Partner Says NO: Pressured Sex & Date Rape by Scott A. Johnson (1992). $6.50.

From Trauma to Understanding: A Guide for Parents of Children with Sexual Behavior Problems by William D. Pithers, Alison S. Gray, Carolyn Cunningham, & Sandy Lane (1993). $5.

Empathy and Compassionate Action: Issues & Exercises: A Workbook for Clients in Treatment by Robert Freeman-Longo, Laren Bays, & Euan Bear (1996). Fourth workbook in a series of four for adult sex offenders. $12.

When Your Wife Says No: Forced Sex in Marriage by Fay Honey Knopp (1994). $7.

Female Adolescent Sexual Abusers: An Exploratory Study of Mother-Daughter Dynamics with Implications for Treatment by Marcia T. Turner & Tracey N. Turner (1994). $18.

Protocol for Phallometric Assessment: A Clinician's Guide by Deloris T. Roys & Pat Roys (1994). $10.

Assessments of Sex Offenders by Measures of Erectile Response: Psychometric Properties and Decision Making by William D. Murphy & Howard Barbaree (1988; updated for Safer Society & bound 1994). $10.

Who Am I & Why Am I in Treatment? A Guided Workbook for Clients in Evaluation and Beginning Treatment by Robert Freeman-Longo & Laren Bays (1988; 8th printing 1997). First workbook in a series of four for adult sex offenders. Also available in Spanish. $12.

Why Did I Do It Again? Understanding My Cycle of Problem Behaviors by Laren Bays & Robert Freeman-Longo (1989; 6th printing 1997). Second in the series. $12.

How Can I Stop? Breaking My Deviant Cycle by Laren Bays, Robert Freeman-Longo, & Diane Montgomery-Logan (1990; 5th printing 1997). Third in the series. $12.

The Relapse Prevention Workbook for Youth in Treatment by Charlene Steen (1993). $15.

The Safer Society Press is part of The Safer Society Foundation, Inc., a 501(c)3 nonprofit national agency dedicated to the prevention and treatment of sexual abuse. We publish additional books, audiocassettes, and training videos related to the treatment of sexual abuse. To receive a catalog of our complete listings, please check the box on the order form (next page) and mail it to the address listed or call us at (802) 247-3132. For more information on the Safer Society Foundation, Inc., visit our website at http://www.safersociety.org.

ORDER FORM

Date:_____

All books shipped via United Parcel Service.
Please include a street location for shipping
as we cannot ship to a Post Office address.

SHIPPING ADDRESS:

Name and/or Agency _____

Street Address (no PO boxes)_____

City _____ State _____ Zip _____

BILLING ADDRESS (if different from shipping address):

Address _____

City _____ State _____ Zip _____

Daytime phone (____)_____   P.O.#_____

Visa or MasterCard #_____ Exp. Date _____

Signature (for credit card order) _____

☐ Do not add me to your mailing list.

QTY	TITLE	UNIT PRICE	TOTAL COST

SUBTOTAL	
VT RESIDENTS ADD SALES TAX	
SHIPPING (SEE BELOW)	
TOTAL	

All prices subject to change without notice.
No returns.

Bulk discounts available, please inquire.
All orders must be prepaid.
Make checks payable to:
SAFER SOCIETY PRESS

Phone orders accepted with MasterCard or Visa.
Call (802) 247-3132.

Mail to:

Safer Society Press
PO Box 340, Brandon VT 05733-0340

Shipping and Handling

1–5 items	$5	16–20 items	$20
6–10 items	$10	21–25 items	$25
11–15 items	$15	26–30 items	$30

31+ items $35
call for quote on rush orders